Lesley Rimmer and Jennie Popay

ısional paper
ber 10

Employment trends and the family

Study Commission on the Family

This occasional paper, like all those in the series, represents views of the authors and not necessarily those of the Study Commission.

The Authors

Lesley Rimmer is a Research Officer with the Study Commission on the Family. She is also author of **Families Focus**

Jennie Popay is a Research Officer with the Study Commission on the Family.

Acknowledgements

This paper was prepared for the Study Commission's work party on 'Work and the Family'. We would like to thank it Chairman, Sara Morrison, and members for their comment Our thanks also go to all those who have commented and their help. We would particularly like to thank Louie Burg Heather Joshi, Val Mason, Ceridwen Roberts and Clare Sh And also our colleagues at the Study Commission, Lynne Feetham, Chris Rossiter and Malcolm Wicks.

Responsibility for any errors remains ours.

Published by the
Study Commission on the Family
3 Park Road, London NW1 6XN
Telephone 01-486 8211 or 8212

Copyright September, 1982
Study Commission on the Family

ISBN 0-907051-11-1

Designed by
Ivor Kamlish FSIAD and Associates

Printed in England by
Witley Press Ltd, Hunstanton

Contents

Figures

Tables

Tables or figures with HMSO copyright have been reproduced with the permission of the Controller of Her Majesty's Stationery Office.

Figure 5 and table 7 have been reproduced with the permission of the Editor of Employment Gazette.

5

Members of the Working Party on Wo and the Family

Sara Morrison (Chairman)

Commission members:
Peter Mandelson
Usha Prashar, Runnymede Trust
Robert Rapoport, Institute of Family
and Environmental Research

Outside members:
Ron Barrowclough, Equal Opportunities Commission
Gerald Dennis, BAT Industries, PLC
Peter Jackson, University of Leicester
Peter Jacques, Trades Union Congress
Chris Patten, MP
Chris Pond, Low Pay Unit
Alan Robertson, Imperial Chemical Industries PLC
Sue Slipman, National Union of Public Employees

Foreword

Traditionally, work and the family tend to be kept in different compartments. Similarly, economic issues and social policy questions are considered by different groups of academics and researchers, different interest groups and separate government departments. But all this now seems to be changing and, certainly, the pace of development defies this compartmentalism.

For a variety of reasons there is a growing interest in the relationship between family issues and the world of work. Perhaps most significantly, a large proportion of women now have, or want to have paid employment outside the home. This has led to a debate about both maternity and paternity provisions and other aspects relating to the family responsibilities of employees. Many obvious major social changes are affecting both employment and the family. Also high levels of unemployment, technological change and the 'future of work' debate are all key issues affecting employment and changing family needs.

As part of its work, the Study Commission on the Family set up a working party to consider some of these dilemmas. The working party members were drawn from industry, and commerce, the academic world and from other broad interest groups. 'Employment Trends and the Family' is the result of our discussions. It is written by the Study Commission's two Research Officers and is not a 'final report' in the conventional sense. All of the working party members are not necessarily in agreement with everything in the document. They are all agreed that it should be published as a contribution to the debate on a subject which will grow in importance and which directly or indirectly concerns virtually every aspect of future economic and social policy.

Sara Morrison
Chairman, Working Party on Work and the Family
Study Commission on the Family

Introduction

Much has been written about the changing nature of
employment and there is also a growing literature on 'the
family', but there have been few attempts to relate these two
areas together in a comprehensive way[1]. This paper tries to
integrate a description of trends in employment and the labour
market with an analysis of the effects of these trends on 'the
family'. And, conversely, it analyses trends in family structures
and functions as they affect labour supply — that is, the
amount people work — and the nature of the work which
people are able and willing to undertake. The focus of the
paper is on Britain in the early 1980s but many of the
problems and issues raised in the paper are common to a
number of countries and where possible we indicate how our
experience differs from that of other nations.

The paper looks both backwards and forwards: it assesses the
impact of recent trends and speculates about the future. It
highlights the uncertainties surrounding future projections of
both the total level of employment and the nature of 'work'
and the complexity of the relationships between employment
and families.

We analyse in some detail the trends in employment and the
labour market over the last fifty years or so, and highlight
particularly the growing importance of women in the
workforce. Just after the Second World War, women were
only one in three of the labour force, and the vast majority of
working women were unmarried. Today, two out of every five
workers are women, with married women outnumbering
unmarried women two to one. And indeed, two fifths of the
female workforce are working parents, as are two fifths of the
male workforce. We also note the parallel growth of part time
work and examine the shifting balance of employment
between sectors. From this 'macro' level we move to a more
'micro' level and describe some important variants in working
patterns — shiftwork, self employment, double job holding,
homeworking and so on.

Unemployment has emerged as a major feature of the
employment scene in the latter part of the 1970s. We chart the

trends in unemployment and show how experience differs between localities and regions. We then consider the spatial dimension of these trends: where have jobs been created, an where are they being lost? Some of the highest levels of unemployment are experienced in the inner cities: some inn areas in Liverpool, for example, having some three times the national average level of unemployment, and we note particularly the employment problems of such inner city are Later in the paper we consider the implications of unemployment for families.

Having described some of the more important trends we mo on to consider the future, both in terms of labour supply an in terms of the changing demand for labour and the nature (work which the diffusion of new technologies may bring.

Finally we bring these issues together. We look at the life cy of family responsibilities — the changing demands of childre ageing parents and spouses — and how these affect people's ability to undertake paid employment. We look, as far as is possible, at the way in which employment decisions are reached within the family and the way in which changes in (individual's employment behaviour may affect that of other family members. We also consider the ways in which familie are themselves changing — how divorce, remarriage, increasi numbers of one parent families and the ageing of the population are affecting employment patterns.

Having looked at the way in which family membership and responsibilities relate to employment behaviour we move or consider how employment itself affects families and individuals within families. Employment has many diverse effects on families, but one major link between employmen and well-being is through incomes. Employment incomes ar the largest component of personal incomes, and much of th social security system is linked to employment status and earnings. We show that family needs over the life cycle do n necessarily match the patterns of resources provided by the labour market and suggest that the income maintenance system is responding inadequately to changing family patte and trends in employment.

Paid employment is not only a source of income and employment benefits, it also provides intrinsic rewards. Conversely, some of the patterns of employment and unemployment that we describe may have unintended, negative effects on individual and family well being. This lir closely with an individual's physical and mental health, and we explore the 'social' consequences of employment and unemployment which are so often neglected.

Finally, we assess the implications of our analysis for policy. Striking the right balance between work and home, and accommodating the tensions and strains which arise are obviously problems which are solved by individuals in their daily lives. But society sets the framework within which such individual adjustments are made[2]. We conclude by indicating some issues for future debate and by highlighting some initiatives which might be valuable.

Throughout the paper we have made use of a range of published and unpublished sources of information. Although the work/family nexus has been of interest for a number of years, it is only recently that developments in social statistics have allowed the relationships to be more adequately explored. Yet even today there are dark areas where the statistical searchlight has yet to fall. We are certainly not alone in wishing to emphasise the crucial role that relevant information should play in the formulation and evaluation of policy[3].

The purpose of the paper

It will be evident from our review of recent trends in the relationship between employment and the family that there are many areas of rapid change and many controversial issues. These involve different perceptions of existing and future trends and different value stances. Our purpose has not been to resolve these differences or to take a particular view of them: rather we have tried to present the available evidence on these changes, to outline the dilemmas to which they give rise, and to inform current and future debates.

Part 1

Recent trends

In this part of the paper we discuss recent trends in employment, labour supply and unemployment. We note particularly the changing composition of the labour force and the increasing significance of part time work. The labour force includes both those who are employed and those who are unemployed but seeking work. We describe both trends in employment and unemployment and analyse the former by sector, industry and occupation. The major focus of the paper is the period from 1921 onwards, although this date is in itself arbitrary. In a number of areas we focus more specifically on the trends from 1970 onwards.

The labour force

The 'labour force' is a shorthand term for all those either in work or seeking work. It includes therefore employees in employment, the self employed, HM Forces, both the registered and unregistered unemployed, and unemployed workers prevented from seeking work by temporary sickness.

The potential size of the labour force depends on the size of the population, on the age structure and on the willingness of various groups to work. Conventions about the ages at which people enter and leave the labour force — particularly school leaving and retirement age — obviously affect the number of people in the labour force, and both these ages have changed over the period. Overall the population below school leaving age has fallen since 1921, from about 28 per cent to 23 per cent of the total population. And the population over retirement age has risen from about 6 per cent to 15 per cent of the population. In total, therefore, the groups of 'working age' have fallen from 66 per cent to 63 per cent of the population[1]

Changes in activity rates, however, have dwarfed the effects of changes in the age structure. These activity rates measure the proportion of the group who are members of the labour force, and there have been three noticeable trends. These are the large decrease in activity rates in the younger age groups, reflecting the raising of the school leaving age and higher participation in post compulsory education; the declining activity rates among older men; and the large increases in activity rates of married women.

In 1921 less than 10 per cent of married women were in the formal labour force. But after the Second World War the proportion of married women in paid employment rose rapidly and continuously, and by 1979 nearly half of all married women were economically active[2]. In aggregate then between 1921 and 1979 the labour force grew from 19.4 million to nearly 26 million — an increase of some 34 per cen This represented, however, a fairly constant proportion of th total population being just over 45 per cent in 1921, 47 per cent in 1976 and 48 per cent in 1979[3].

Changes in activity rates have been the most significant feature of the changes in labour supply, and the explanation the changing activity rates of women — particularly married women — is discussed later. Even if the very low 1921 activit rates had remained unchanged, there would have been an increase of nearly 50 per cent in the number of married women in the labour force due to the rise in the number of women of marriageable age, earlier marriage, and a greater likelihood that women would marry. But if their activity rate had remained unchanged there would be some 4.36 million **fewer** married women currently in the labour force. On the other hand, there would be 1.1 million more young people ir the labour force today and an almost equivalent number of older men[4]. Recently, however, activity rates for older workers have declined as we document later.

While changes in the age structure have had a much smaller impact, they can have important implications for employmen prospects in the short term. Over the next two to three years for example, the low birth rate of the First World War means that fewer men will be reaching retirement age and the numb of women reaching 60 will also be falling as a result of low birth rates in the 1920's. But while the numbers reaching retirement age are low, the numbers leaving school are near record levels because of the high birth rates in the 1960s. In combination, these two trends will lead to an increase of som 3 per cent in the working age population between 1981 and 1986[5].

One further feature which can affect the size of the labour force is immigration, and at particular times immigration has been encouraged to remove labour or skill shortages. Today some 6 per cent of the labour force were born outside the U with just over 2 per cent from the New Commonwealth and Pakistan[6]. The activity rates of males of ethnic minority origin differ little from those of males of white origin for those aged over 35, whilst the activity rates of younger ethnic minority males are lower, because of the large number of students. Amongst ethnic minority married women, though in general activity rates are lower than those of other married women, there is considerable variation between groups. West Indian married women, of all ages, are more likely than any other group of married women to be economically active[7].

As a result of the changes described above there have been substantial changes in the composition of the labour force, and it is to this that we now turn.

As Figure 1 shows, in 1921 women were only one in three of the labour force, and the vast majority of working women were unmarried. Today two out of every five workers are women, and married women workers now outnumber unmarried ones by about two to one. Overall then, one quarter of the labour force are married women and about half of these can be expected to be caring for at least one dependent child[8].

Figure 1. The composition of the labour force

1921
3.8%
25.7%
70.5%

1951
11.8%
19.0%
69.2%

1971
23.1%
13.5%
63.4%

1979
25.9%
13.4%
60.6%

Married women

Non-married women

Men

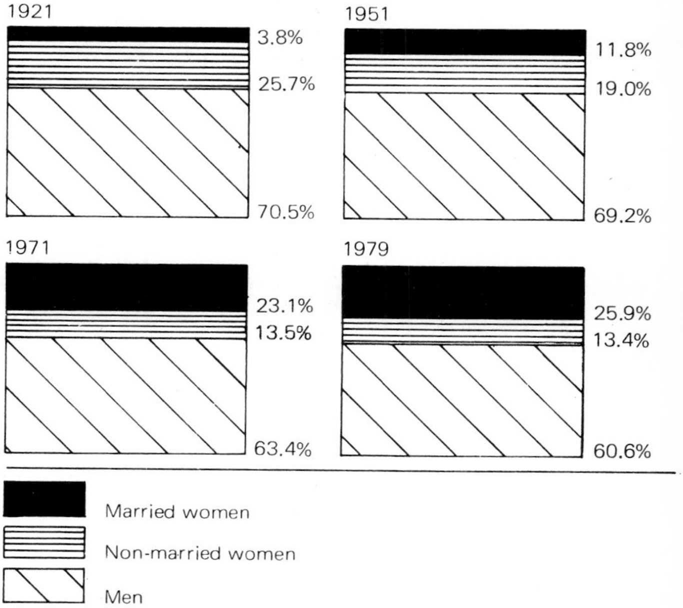

Source: RCDIW Report number 8 and Background paper number 1 to Cmnd 8093. Table 2.6

Until very recently information about the family situations
workers or of the unemployed has been incomplete, focusse
primarily on the number of dependent children for whom
women were responsible. But new data from the General
Household Survey show the current situation more adequa
and we discuss this in some detail later.

Trends in total employment

Having described the major trends in the composition of th
labour force we move on to describe the trends in
employment. Overall, employment grew from 21 million ir
1959 to some 22.3 million in 1979, but it has subsequently
fallen back to 20.7 million[9]. As table 1 shows the trends ha
been different for men and women. Male employment has
fallen from 1965 onwards, whereas women's employment
continued to increase until the most recent downturn.

Table 1. Employees in employment millions

	Total*	Men	Women	Women as % of total
1921	17.4	12.1	5.2	30
1931	19.0	13.1	5.8	31
1951	21.0	14.2	6.6	31
1959	21.0	13.8	7.2	33
1965	22.6	14.5	8.1	36
1975	22.2	13.3	9.0	40
1978	22.2	13.1	9.1	41
1979	22.3	13.0	9.3	42
1980	22.0	12.8	9.2	42
1981	20.7	12.0	8.7	42

Source: see reference[10]
*figures may not add due to rounding

It has been suggested that there were three distinct phases
employment trends from 1959 to the mid 1970's[11]. Firstl
the period 1959-1966 was one of expansion with full
employment. Then the immediate pre and post devaluatio
phase of 1967-71 was a period of gradually rising
unemployment with sharp falls in male employment and a
halt to the growth in female employment. And finally the
Conservative Government's dash for growth in 1972-73 le
a rapid increase in the number of women in employment,
to a slowing down in the decline of male employment.

After the recession of 1975 when employment fell by nea
400,000 in the space of 18 months, the employed labour

began to grow slowly and at the end of 1979 there were 400,000 more male employees in employment than there were in 1970[12]. In the three years to June 1979 total employment increased by 250,000 but over the year to June 1980, male employment fell by 272,000 and female employment fell by 135,000[13], and by December 1980 employment was down to 21.3 million. Subsequently it has fallen to 20.7 million (June 1981) — and thus the total number of employees was almost 7½ per cent below the level two years earlier[14]. And this decline in employment has been paralleled by a substantial increase in unemployment which is detailed later.

In discussing trends in employment and the labour force we have used figures compiled on the basis of full time and part time workers being counted as equal. In fact a very substantial part of the increase in married women's employment has been in part time work, and to that extent such labour force and employment totals overstate the growth of actual labour input. If part time working, changes in hours worked and increased holidays, are taken into account, the picture looks rather different. For example, the Unit for Manpower Studies has estimated that while the labour force grew by 5 per cent over the period 1961 to 1971 there was a loss in terms of aggregate annual hours worked of about 5 per cent. In more concrete terms this loss was equivalent to just over one million manual men working 1961 average annual hours[15]. Indeed, part time employment, usually defined in Britain as 30 hours a week or less, has been a growing aspect of the employment picture with 20 per cent of the total labour force working part time in 1979[16]. We return to this issue in a later section.

Trends in employment by sector, by occupation and by industry

The trends in total employment described earlier subsume differences between sectors — agriculture, industry or services — between industries and between occupations. The distinctions between these categories are in some cases not very helpful, but they are often referred to and we describe the trends in employment in each of them.

Associated with the increasing number of women in the labour force has been the increasing importance of employment in service sectors and occupations, and in non manual rather than manual jobs. Employment in both the secondary (manufacturing) and tertiary (service) sectors has increased at the expense of employment in the primary sector, which now accounts for a minute proportion of the employed population[17]. A more recent trend — characterised as deindustrialisation — is the decline in the importance of manufacturing employment and the corresponding increase the proportion of total employment in services.

Such overall trends, however, conceal a more complex realit Firstly there are problems of definition —
"virtually all standard employment data relate labour to the product of its activities; thus a typist working in a bank is attributed on this basis to the banking sector. However, employment data based on occupations would clearly indic that many employment activities are the same whether classed as tertiary or secondary activities[18] ".

Secondly, the trend has been somewhat different for men a women and, linked to this, there have been differences between full and part time employment.

Thirdly, while it is desirable to analyse changes in the occupational distribution of employment there are particul, problems in describing long term trends: occupational classifications change fairly frequently, and there are severa ways in which occupations can be grouped. The Royal Commission on the Distribution of Income and Wealth, for example, used a classification of 'occupational classes' base(on the nature of work and the level of skill[19]. Their analysi showed a number of important trends, of which the most pronounced was the shift from manual to non-manual occupations.

In 1921 14 per cent of male employees were in non-manual occupations, by 1951 this was 20 per cent and by 1971 it v 31 per cent[20]. Within the non-manual occupations, employment in professional and managerial occupations ro: much faster than that in clerical occupations, and within manual occupations there was a shift from the less skilled t(the more skilled occupations.

A similar shift to non-manual employment is evident for women. The number of women in manual occupations has declined absolutely and proportionately. A large part of thi fall is due to the decline in numbers employed in domestic service (from 1.3 million in 1921 to 239,000 in 1971), and later decline in employment in textile manufacture. For women, however, employment in clerical occupations grew fast up to 1971. Whereas in 1921 and 1931 men outnumbe women in clerical occupations, by 1951 positions had been reversed and the predominance of women in clerical occupations increased up to 1971.

18

There is no exact connection between industry and occupation in terms of the main Census classification of occupations. Nonetheless the changes in employment by **industry** which were analysed for the Royal Commission also showed a massive increase in service employment, both in absolute terms and as a proportion of total employment. In the decade to 1980, employment in the service industries grew by over 1.5 million. Much of this employment growth in services is a reflection of the growth of public employment — indeed, 71 per cent of the total increase in employment in services between 1961 and 1975 was in the central and local government sectors[21]. But there has now been a marked change in trend. In the first and second quarters of 1980 the number of employees in the service industries fell by 30,000 each quarter, and by 100,000 in the fourth quarter, giving a total decline of about 3¼ per cent from the level of employment at the end of 1979[22].

Employment in manufacturing industry increased (other than in textiles and clothing) between 1931 and 1961, fell slightly between 1961 and 1971, and has fallen much more rapidly since. Indeed, by August 1981, employment in manufacturing industry was nearly 1.2 million or 16½ per cent below the level at June 1976[23], and such 'deindustrialisation' has become an important feature of the current recession.

Self employment

In addition to employees we need to consider self employment. In 1921 some 10 per cent of the labour force were self employed, but by 1979 this had fallen to 8 per cent or some 1,795,000 people. A higher proportion of men than women are self employed, 10 per cent compared to 5 per cent, and the decline in self employment has been more significant for women, from 8 per cent to 5 per cent, than for men from 11 to 10 per cent.[24]

Self employed workers are concentrated in a narrow range of occupations and industries, and indeed 85 per cent of them are in five industrial groups. These are agriculture, forestry and fishing, construction, retail distribution, professional and scientific services, and miscellaneous services. Of these, construction accounts for nearly a quarter of the self employed, and retail distribution a fifth[25]. In a number of cases those who are self employed may have more than one occupation. What information we have on the extent of self employment is still not totally reliable, and indeed, the whole question of the extent and nature of such employment is tie up with a growing interest in the 'hidden' and 'informal' economies[26].

Working patterns

Having discussed employment in broad numerical terms we now move on to consider trends in working patterns. We discuss part time working, homeworking, double job holdin and the hours people work. Some commentators argue that these working patterns are best understood using a model o 'labour market segmentation'[27].

It is argued that the labour market is divided into at least tw — relatively distinct — sub markets, one a 'core' labour mar and one an 'outer' or secondary labour market. This line of reasoning suggests that in the core labour market, occupatic are characterised by high wages, job security and good worl conditions, with on-the-job training and low staff turnover. The outer labour market, on the other hand, consists of firr with low wage levels, poor working conditions and job instability. The core labour market jobs are likely to be fill by 'prime age, white males', with some specific skills, and t outer labour market jobs by variously described 'marginal workers' — young and old workers, women, those with littl skill, and ethnic minority workers. Such duality can also ex it is suggested, **within** the same firm — where groups of 'hig disposable' labour are employed alongside a group in which there is longer term investment in training and greater provision of career opportunities.

This segmentation can be seen to result partly from emplo need to retain both a stable and a more disposable element their workforce, to give some flexibility and to match fluctuating product demand. Equally, union boundaries an the extent of unionisation, may emphasise divisions betwee groups of workers, and foster greater security of employm for some groups rather than others. Some groups of worke may find their effective choice of work constrained by the family responsibilities. We argue later that this model fits particularly well the case of married women with children, who are often concentrated in low grade, low paid and lov status jobs which simply add to the pressures upon them[28] many cases, employment in this 'secondary' labour market part time employment and it is to this that we now turn.

Part time work

Part time work has been a growing part of the employment picture. One in five of the employed labour force works part time. But such work is predominantly done by women — and indeed 90 per cent of part time workers are women, of whom nine out of ten are married[29]. In addition, 14 per cent of part time workers are over retirement age and, in contrast to the working age groups, two-fifths of these are men[30]. If we consider the male and female workforces separately, then over 40 per cent of women workers work part time and this is true of 70 per cent of mothers with dependent children. For mothers with a pre school child, this proportion rises to nearly 80 per cent[31]. In contrast only 4 per cent of male workers are part timers and six out of ten of these are over retirement age[32].

As we describe later, part time work is often 'chosen' because of family responsibilities, and in parallel with the increasing number of married women in the female labour force, an increasing proportion of all women have worked part time. One estimate suggests that 20-25 per cent of the female workforce were engaged in part time work in 1960, 30 per cent in 1970 and 42 per cent in 1979[33]. By international standards, a high proportion of British women work part time. But the definition of part time work varies between countries — it is 25 hours or less in the Netherlands — and such international comparisons cannot, therefore be pressed too far[34]. Equally, as we note later, the actual hours worked by part timers may vary considerably and indeed may have changed over time.

We have shown that the growth in part time employment was linked with the growth in service employment. Indeed, between 1961 and 1971 the growth in service employment was due to the growth in the number of female workers by nearly 1.2 million and the indications are that almost all of this was in part time work. More recently service employment has declined and in some instances part timers have been particularly vulnerable. Education is a case in point. At the beginning of the 1970s there was one part time teacher for every 8.5 full time teachers in maintained primary and secondary schools in England and Wales, 90 per cent of whom were female[35]. By 1979, however, there was only one part time teacher for every 14 full time teachers and it is suggested that the cuts in education budgets were continuing to affect part timers disproportionately. We comment in detail at a later stage on the value of part time employment for those

with family responsibilities, but note here that any decline
part time employment opportunities may have significant
implications for families.

Shiftworking

Part time work is often linked to shift systems. Shiftwork
is, however, in some ways difficult to define since it can in
a number of different working patterns, including staggere
day work, alternating or double day systems, permanent n
shifts, split shifts and so on. In addition, various groups,
especially part time workers, often work unsocial hours as
their normal working times[36].

Available evidence suggests that shiftworking has been
increasing over the last thirty years. In 1954 12 per cent o
manual workers in manufacturing industry worked shifts.
1968 the National Board of Prices and Incomes estimated
some 25 per cent of all adult manual workers in manufact
undertook some form of shiftwork (22 per cent for all
industries). More recently, estimates suggest that this
proportion has increased only slightly to about 26 per cen
However, since shiftworking is one way in which employe
ensure the continuous use of expensive plant and machine
or match staffing to peak demand periods, such patterns o
working may be expected to increase, as pressures mount
reduce costs, and with the introduction of microelectronic
technology. The consequences — both economic and socia
of shiftwork are discussed later, but it is important to note
that working shifts is one way in which family members ca
overcome problems of child care: one parent works, while
other looks after the children.

Homeworking

Another response to the problems of combining paid work
with family responsibilities is homeworking, and indeed fc
many homeworkers alternative employment is ruled out b
the need to care virtually full time for children or other
dependants. Many types of workers can be considered as
homeworkers: a strict definition might include only those
'working in or from their homes for an employer who sup
the work and is responsible for marketing and selling the
results', whereas a broader definition could encompass chi
minders and other self employed workers[38].

Between the 1921 and 1971 Censuses the number of people who reported themselves as working at home rose from one-quarter to 1.5 million — or from 1.4 per cent to 6 per cent of the labour force. Within this an unknown number are actually 'home-workers' in terms of the strict definition given above. Townsend for example estimated that in 1968-9 some 1.15 million people worked at home; of these 300,000 were employees providing services and between 100,000 and 150,000 were doing work for a contractor[39]. And more recently the Select Committee on Employment has estimated that between 100,000 and 400,000 women are working at home[40]. Until the results of the special section in the 1981 Labour Force Survey and of a Department of Employment survey of 'Women and Employment' become available, however, such estimates of homeworkers are little more than 'guesstimates'. It would seem that the advantages to employers of this type of work and rising unemployment among women will mean that homeworking may well increase in the future.

Double job holding

Not everyone has only one job — and indeed, double job holding may be a growing dimension to the labour market, partly as a response to financial pressure or to the inability to find one full time job. It is also linked to the rise of the informal economy[41]. The 1978 General Household Survey showed that 3 per cent of all workers had more than one job, and this rose to 4 per cent in the 25-44 age group. For both employees and the self employed, the second job was more likely to be as an employee rather than in self employment.[42] It would be valuable to have more information about the nature of these second jobs and in particular it is worth noting that a substantial majority of women's second jobs are of the mail order agent type, which can be fitted in flexibly with home responsibilities.

Hours of work

The basic number of hours people work each week has fallen almost continuously over the last hundred years. The trend abated during the Second World War, but since the 1960s reductions have been taking place steadily. Perhaps the most important change has been the general introduction of the 40 hour normal working week in the 1960s, but there have also been reductions in hours beyond this for certain groups. On the other hand, British workers — in contrast to their continental counterparts — still work considerable amounts of overtime. In 1980 employees in manufacturing industry worked 11.5 million hours overtime per week or an average 8.3 hours per worker per week.[43].

The result of these two trends is that in 1980 the average working week for male workers was 43 hours and 38 hours full time female workers[44]. For men, these hours are comparable to those in other European countries, except France and the Irish Republic where weekly hours are high but they are substantially less for British women than for th European counterparts[45]. As we noted above, a higher proportion of women in Britain work part time, and there i substantial variation in hours actually worked within this. T 1977 Labour Force Survey, for example, showed that one i eight part time married women workers worked eight hours less a week and a further quarter worked between nine and sixteen hours[46].

The number of hours which people work is obviously important in determining the amount of time they have available for other roles — as parent, husband, wife or 'care — and for leisure. One response to high levels of unemployment has been the idea of work sharing through reductions in hours, and the effects of such reductions have recently been examined in a number of companies[47]. The study highlights the fact that reductions in working time ca be achieved through shorter working weeks, increases in holiday entitlement, or through changes in overtime workir Equally they can be related to early retirement practices or changes in the age of retirement, and the issues raised by th alternative options are rather different.

The age of retirement is currently the subject of a Select Committee investigation, and we note some of the implications of a shortened working lifetime later in the pap Up to the present time there seems to have been rather mor development of extensions to holiday entitlement, compare with reductions in weekly hours. In 1970, for example, just over 20 per cent of all full time adult male workers had an annual holiday entitlement of four weeks or more. By 1974 this had risen to 36 per cent, and by 1981 it had reached 88 per cent. The levels are similar for full time adult women workers, and evidence suggests that the gaps between manu and non manual workers, and between men and women workers have been narrowed [48].

It may be therefore that the scope for extending increases i holiday entitlement further is rather limited and that, in fut more serious consideration will be given to reducing the working week. Where this happens, the study cited above indicates that there is no automatic increase in employment, and the author concludes that 'The evidence as a whole suggests that the aggregate effect on employment of reductions in working time will be rather small. It would seem unwise to regard these developments as effective methods of reducing unemployment'[49].

A further issue is the extent to which such working hours are flexible, since this is often important in enabling people to integrate their home and work responsibilities.

Unemployment

A prominent feature of employment trends today is the high level of unemployment we are currently experiencing. While levels of unemployment tend to follow a cyclical pattern — with periods of boom and high employment following those of a slump — there is a real concern that there may have been an upward 'shift' in the underlying level of unemployment which will characterise the economy. Yet, despite a widespread belief to the contrary, total **employment** in the past 10 years did not decrease until very recently. There were actually more people working 1979 than in 1970.

But while employment increased the numbers seeking work also increased, and unemployment rates are now higher than at any time in the post war period. Indeed, the current high levels of unemployment have been likened to the period of the 1930s. Between 1921 and 1939, unemployment did not fall below 9 per cent of the labour force in any single year and in 1932 — the trough of the depression — unemployment reached 22 per cent (or 2.8 million people); between 1930 and 1935 it remained above 15 per cent.[50] In individual towns, however, the rates were much higher: 77 per cent of the labour force of Jarrow were out of work in 1933 and at Taff Wells in Wales, it was 82 per cent[51].

In contrast, for most of the post war period, unemployment was generally low: in the 1950s, for example, it seldom exceeded 1.5 per cent. In the 1960s it varied between 1.4 per cent and 2.6 per cent, and it was only in the late 1970s that there were indications of the high levels of unemployment with which the 1980s would start. In 1971, unemployment reached 3.6 per cent and from 1975 it climbed fairly steadily — with some respite in 1978 and 1979 — towards the current

level of over 12 per cent of the labour force, with some 3
million people registered as unemployed[52]. Today it is a s
fact that one in eight of the labour force is unemployed.

The spatial aspects

This overall picture, however, disguises substantial differei
between regions. Certain regions, particularly the north ar
north west of England, as well as Wales and Scotland, hav
persistently higher levels of unemployment than other are
and the differentials remain. Today, when the unemploym
rate in Great Britain is 12.2 per cent, in the North and in
Wales it is 15.9 per cent and 15.7 per cent respectively, th
30 per cent higher than the national average[53]. In contras
9 per cent, the level in the South East is some 26 per cent
below the average. Details of the regional pattern are give
Table 2. **Within** regions there are small areas where levels
unemployment are even higher. In Ebbw Vale, unemploy
is already over 20 per cent, as it is in Irvine; in Consett or
four members of the workforce is unemployed.[54]

Table 2. Unemployment: by region, sex and duration

	% of Great Britain total		1981 unemployment rates			
Region	Employees in employ- ment Sept 1981	Unemploy- ment 1981	Total	Male	Female	% total unempl out of v over 1 y Jan 198
Great Britain	100.0	100.0	11.1	13.4	7.8	29.2
South East	33.5	23.1	8.0	10.0	5.2	23.3
East Anglia	3.1	2.5	9.1	11.0	6.2	24.1
South West	7.3	6.3	9.9	11.9	7.1	26.2
West Midlands	9.5	11.9	13.5	16.1	9.6	33.5
East Midlands	7.0	6.3	10.1	12.3	7.0	29.5
Yorks/Humberside	8.8	9.7	12.1	14.5	8.4	30.3
North West	11.7	14.8	13.7	16.4	9.8	32.3
North	5.5	7.7	15.0	17.7	10.8	34.1
England	86.3	82.3	10.8	13.1	7.5	28.9
Wales	4.4	5.9	14.5	16.9	10.9	31.8
Scotland	9.3	11.7	13.6	15.9	10.4	29.8
Great Britain	100.0	100.0	11.1	13.4	7.8	29.2

Source: Employment Gazette. January 1982 Tables 1.5 and 2.3,
February 1982 Table 2.6.

A particularly important spatial aspect, and one to which
increasing attention is being given, is the employment situ
in inner city areas. This cannot be given the attention it
deserves in this paper, but we can note some of the dimer
of the problem.

Since the late 1950s, the inner areas of conurbations have been in decline, and there has been a move towards growth on their peripheries. Between 1961 and 1976, the inner areas of six large conurbations (London, Birmingham, Merseyside, Greater Manchester, Tyneside and Clydeside) lost over a million jobs — or almost 20 per cent of their 1961 employment. As a result, unemployment rose from 3.7 per cent of the labour force to 13.7 per cent, or twice as much as in other areas.[55] The 1960s also saw a rising exodus of population from the inner city areas, but not sufficiently high to offset the loss of employment opportunities. In the 1970s, employment continued to decline and by the mid-1970s the unemployment problem in inner cities equalled the regional unemployment problem in seriousness.

Both the population drift from the inner cities and the rise in unemployment continued into the late 1970s. The preliminary results of the 1981 Census show that every large city in Britain has suffered substantial population losses since 1971 and in most instances these affected inner areas disproportionately. The inner boroughs in London together lost half a million people, with Kensington and Chelsea losing 26 per cent of its population[56]. But despite these massive outflows of population, unemployment has continued to increase and to be at much higher levels than in more favoured areas.

Again, 1981 Census data give some indication of the scale of the problem. In Merseyside unemployment among men of working age stands at 17.8 per cent. In Liverpool it is 21.6 per cent, but in the 'special area' wards of Liverpool it rises to 23.1 per cent. In some individual wards — Abercromby for example — the rate climbs to over 35 per cent[57].

Figure 2 illustrates both the higher rates of unemployment within inner areas generally and the even higher levels suffered by non white workers. In general ethnic minority workers experience higher rates of unemployment than their white counterparts, and the incidence is strikingly high for certain groups, for example young West Indians. The most recent information is from the National Dwelling and Housing Survey for 1977. At that time the rate of unemployment for minority groups was 9.6 per cent compared with 5.2 per cent for the general population[58]. To some extent minorities are more vulnerable than whites because they are concentrated within age groups, and skill levels that are themselves especially vulnerable. But these problems are compounded in inner city areas, which are the principal centres of the Asian and West Indian communities[59].

Figure 2. Inner city unemployment

Male unemployment rates by area of residence (unemployed/ economically active)

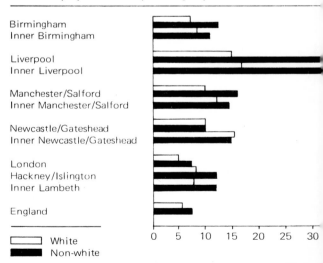

Male unemployment rates by ethnic group and area of residence

Source: CSO Inner Cities in England, Social Trends 10, HMSO Figure B3.

Unemployment: by age and duration

We explore later in the paper the correlates — both econom and social — of unemployment. Here we merely paint a br picture of the current situation and the way in which this has been changing. Two aspects are of particular importance: the high levels of unemployment among young people, and the increasing proportion of the unemployed who have been out of work for long periods.

While unemployment of all durations has increased, there has been a particularly pronounced increase in the proportion unemployed for over a year. In 1972 this group accounted for about one sixth of the total unemployed, but by 1981 it had risen to about one quarter[60]. Worryingly over one in twenty of men registered as unemployed have been out of work for three years or more[61]. Similarly youth unemployment has become more significant. Nearly one fifth of the unemployed in January 1982 were aged under 20 and unemployment rates for young people are particularly high in some areas[62]. Again the ethnic minority population is especially at risk, since it has a higher proportion of workers in the younger age groups than the rest of the population.

Table 3. Duration of unemployment by age Great Britain October 1981

Age group	Unemployment rate	%* unemployed for over 1 year	%** unemployed for over 3 years
Under 18	25.0	4.0	—
18-19	23.0	16.2	0.2
20-24	18.3	23.6	1.9
25-34	11.4	26.0	3.5
35-44	7.7	29.2	5.8
45-54	7.2	34.0	9.8
55-59	8.9	37.9	12.6
60+	14.9	43.4	13.8
All ages	12.2	25.9	4.9

Source: Employment Gazette November 1981 Table 2.6

* percentage of the unemployed in each age group who have been unemployed for more than one year.

**percentage of the unemployed in each age group who have been unemployed for more than three years.

Tables 3 and 4 document the dimensions of the unemployment problem, and highlight the incidence and composition of unemployment. However, the picture of unemployment presented by these figures is deficient in at least one important respect. Currently in Britain statistics of unemployment are derived from the process of registering for unemployment benefits. Not all those who are unemployed register and not all those who register are entitled to benefit. Non registration would not pose too much of a problem in interpreting the statistics of unemployment if it represented a constant proportion of those out of work and seeking a job. But thi not the case: as unemployment rises people become less hopeful of finding employment and fail to register — espec where there is no financial benefit in doing so, as is the cas for many married women. Conversely, when jobs are plent people are more likely to register.

But how significant is such non registration and what are tl implications of it? A picture of the extent of non registrati can be obtained from the General Household Survey (GHS This shows that in 1980, 89 per cent of unemployed males registered as unemployed. In contrast only 57 per cent of

Table 4. Percentage of total unemployed in each age group Great B

	Under 18	18-19	20-24	25-34	35-44	45-54	55-59	60+	All ages
1982 (Jan)	7.5	10.3	19.6	22.3	13.3	12.0	7.3	7.6	100.0
1978 (Jan)	9.1	9.4	18.6	21.8	13.2	12.1	6.4	9.4	100.0

Source: Employment Gazette February 1982 Table 2.6.

unemployed married women were registered. This proporti has increased rapidly in recent years, however, from 52 per cent in 1979 and 47 per cent in 1977, partly as a result of changes in the regulations governing national insurance contributions and benefits[63].

Not all of those who are registered, on the other hand, are seeking work; 11 per cent of men who were registered in 1 described themselves as economically inactive, and this wa true of 23 per cent of married women. On balance, howeve especially for women, figures of registered unemployment are more likely to understate rather than overstate the num of people wishing to work. in this sense then, figures of registered unemployment understate the true extent of unemployment, and indeed some estimates put this 'true' as high as 4 million already[64]. In addition both employmei creation programmes and the short time working compensation scheme are reducing the number who might otherwise be unemployed.

In addition to the non registered unemployed who are seel work, there are an unknown number of workers who are currently 'discouraged' from seeking employment. It is thought that these are mainly married women and men who have retired early[65]. If job opportunities in general improved, or if a job presented itself they might well re-enter the labour market. Thus the pool of potential workers is not fixed but varies with the level and nature of available job opportunities. Hence, if registered unemployment is to be reduced by, say, half a million, total **employment** may have to increase by substantially more than this.

Similar problems arise when trying to measure the extent of long term unemployment which is now normally defined as having been unemployed for over a year. Official figures for duration are counted from the date of last registration. The omission of individuals who leave the register for short spells, but who in total may have experienced long, interrupted spells of unemployment may therefore significantly underestimate the extent of what is perhaps the single most important indicator of the impact of unemployment.

Finally we turn to an important dimension of unemployment, but one which is too often overlooked — the family dimension. A recognition of the impact of unemployment on the **family,** rather than on the unemployed as individuals, is welcome as a counter-weight to normal measures of the 'problem' of unemployment, defined solely in terms of the numbers registered as unemployed. So, while three million workers may be registered as unemployed, perhaps two or three times as many **people** may be in families directly experiencing unemployment. When individuals are unemployed, their families experience it with them, and it is important to know whether men and women with dependants are more or less likely to experience unemployment than those without dependants. We discuss in a later section the impact of unemployment on individuals and their families, but it is essential to note some aspects of this question here.

Unemployment and the family: the basic picture

It has been until recently difficult to determine the relative extent to which family heads, or those with dependants, experienced unemployment. Some information has become available recently about the unemployed from two studies: the DHSS cohort study and the MSC study of the unemployed flow, and about the family responsibilities of the labour force from the GHS[66]. But the issue is complicated by whether one looks at the stock of unemployment at one point in time or the flow over time, and whether one is looking at the risk of becoming unemployed or of remaining so.

31

A further crucial distinction is whether it is the **risk** of beiunemployed that is being considered (that is, the incidence
unemployment in a particular group) or the proportion of
total unemployment that a particular group represents (the
composition of unemployment). The distinction is import
for policy making purposes, and the available data from th
1980 General Household Survey is presented in the figures
below.

Figure 3 shows the risk or incidence of unemployment for
males aged 16-64. Six per cent of all such males were
unemployed in 1980. The risk of unemployment for marri
men (5 per cent) was less than for men of all marital statu
(6 per cent), and substantially less than that for single mer
per cent) or for the widowed, divorced and separated (8 p
cent). However, if married men only, are considered the ra
of unemployment for married men with dependent childre
(5 per cent) is higher than for men without children (4 per
cent), and for men with four or more dependent children
nearly two and a half times as great (12 per cent) as for
married men with no children.

**Figure 3. Incidence: rates of unemployment by marital status: mal
aged 16-64 by number of dependent children**

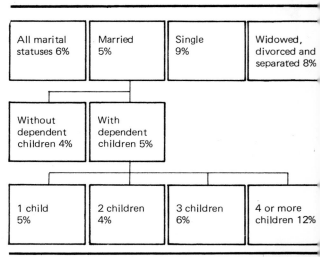

Source: previously unpublished data from the 1980 General House
Survey — equivalent data were published in tables 5.5, 5.8 and 5.9
the General Household Survey 1979 (HMSO) 1981

Figure 3 focusses on the relative risk of unemployment in
various groups, which is clearly affected by age; but it is
perhaps equally important to consider what proportion of

unemployed men are married men, with and without dependent children, single men and so on. This is shown in figure 4.

Figure 4. Composition: percentage of all those unemployed who are of various marital statuses, and dependencies, males aged 16-64

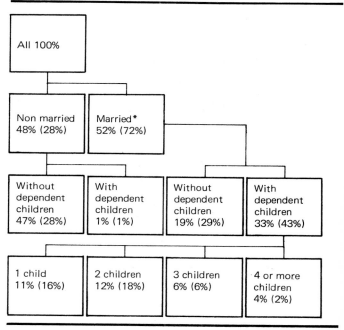

Note: Figures may not add to 100 due to rounding.
Source: Previously unpublished data from the 1980 General Household Survey. Equivalent data were published in table 5.12 of the GHS 1979 (HMSO) 1981.
* the tables refer to men in married couples of working age (ie their wife was in the household and aged 16-59).
Note: Figures in brackets refer to the respective proportions of economically active males. Comparison of these figures to those in the relevant unemployment tree branches can also be used as an index of the relative 'risk' of unemployment.

It can be clearly seen from this that just over half of all unemployed men are married men, and a third are married men with dependent children. Eleven per cent of unemployed men are married men with one child, 12 per cent married men with two children, and 6 per cent are married men with three children. Married men with four or more children, whose risk of being unemployed was more than twice as high as for all married men, represent just 4 per cent of all unemployed men. This focus on the dependants of married men follows the

practice of treating the man as the head of a married coup
family. However, over half of all families with dependent
children now have two earners, and we should be increasi
aware of the impact of women's unemployment on their
families[67]. Equally, the picture presented above is of the
of unemployment — that is those who are unemployed at
point in time. We also need to look at the flow of
unemployment — that is the risk of **becoming** unemploye
and at the composition and risk of long term unemploym

Both the cohort studies seem to suggest that the unmarrie
are more at risk of becoming unemployed. In the DHSS c
the men joining the register tended to be young, and part
because of this men registering were less likely to be marr
than the general population, and of those who were marr
36 per cent had no dependent children[68]. And on the bas
his study Daniel suggests that married men entering
unemployment 'had dependent children in numbers that
if anything, slightly less than those of the working popula
generally'[69].

But if married men with dependent children are less likel
become unemployed, once they are unemployed, are the
more or less likely to stay so than other men? Here Danie
suggests that 'the tendency for married men with a larger
number of children to be over represented among the
unemployed stock is a consequence of longer periods out
work rather than of a greater likelihood of becoming
unemployed'[70]. Certainly the MSC study of the long term
unemployed showed that 58 per cent of them were marri
(two thirds of the men and 27 per cent of the women) ar
over a third had children who were financially dependent
them. For the prime working age groups, 25 to 44 year o
this rose to 64 per cent[71].

How will rising unemployment affect this picture? The
question is a complex one, and the evidence available to
answer it is limited. Between 1966 and 1971, when
unemployment doubled, there was a marked shift towarc
families with dependent children.

More recently, comparison of the data from the 1979 an
1980 General Household Surveys shows little change in t
composition of male unemployment by dependency but
should be noted that in this instance the rate of male
unemployment identified by the GHS rose only from five
six per cent. In addition, recent benefit data raise questic
about changes in composition over the decade 1970-198

However, it remains true that the incidence of unemployment is greater for the heads of large families. In consequence, the proportion of **children** affected by unemployment is higher than the proportion of families. The 1971 Census figures showed that 3.5 per cent of all family heads were out of employment, but 4.9 per cent of all children lived in such families[73]. As the incidence of unemployment is greater for those in the lower socio-economic groups, the proportion of children witnessing unemployment in the family also rises as social class falls. Again the 1971 Census showed that while 8.3 per cent of family heads in social class V were out of work, 15.8 per cent of children in this class experienced unemployment of the head of the family[74]. In December 1980 (the latest available figure) there were ¾ million children experiencing the unemployment of the 'family head'[75].

It is clear then, that a family dimension is developing in the discussion of unemployment and its consequences[76].

Part 2 # Future trends

We have described some of the major trends which have ta
place recently in labour supply and in the nature, pattern
volume of employment. But what of the future?

Employment and labour supply

Projections covering changes in employment are based on
specified assumptions about underlying economic trends,
government policy, the development of technology and th
political, social and institutional environment[1]. They gene
relate to the short term (12-18 months), the medium term
(1-5 years) or the longer term (5-15 years). Obviously the
uncertainties involved and, hence, the unreliability of the
projections increase with time. But officially unemployme
now over 3 million and there is a growing acceptance of th
view that it is likely to remain of this order for a consider
time. This high and rising level of unemployment appears
have had its effects on labour force growth in the past few
years and though the future implications are far from
straightforward, some tentative comments are possible.

During the four years to 1981, current estimates suggest t
the labour force may have actually fallen by approximate
150,000 rather than increasing by the 700,000 thought li
in the 1977 projections for the period[2]. This was despite
increase in the population of working age of the order of
700,000. The decline was due in part to the unprecedente
changes in activity rates of men in the age groups 60-64 a
65-69[3]. Indeed according to GHS data, the proportion of
nearing retirement age — between 60 and 64 — who were
'economically active' fell from 84 per cent to 75 per cent
between 1975 and 1979, and in 1980 by a further 8
percentage points to 67 per cent. Such figures may, howe
overestimate the rate of decline and the latest LFS figure
70 per cent suggests a continuing but slower decline.[4]
However, activity rates amongst older women appear to h
declined sharply, and amongst married women of all ages,
activity rates have 'not only stopped increasing but have a
slipped back from the record levels reached in 1977'[5].

It is not clear whether these declining activity rates are temporary or permanent. It is almost certainly the case that as unemployment has increased faster than projected over the past two years, activity rates have similarly declined faster than projected, and may continue to do so. If the reduced activity rates are temporary, then we might expect some return towards previous levels when the economic situation improves. However, in the case of married women, in addition to the recession, the declining activity rates are also associated with an increased birth rate since 1977. Though the direction of causation here is far from clear, if the birth rate continued to increase then we might expect activity rates amongst women aged 25-34 to decline still further in the future.[6]

Predicting activity rates is a difficult exercise. As we have seen, even over relatively short time periods, they can change dramatically. In the future, they may be affected not only by unemployment but also by changing patterns of family life such as divorce and lone parenthood, issues which are discussed more fully in Part 3.

However, the size and composition of the **population of working age** can be projected with more confidence than activity rates — at least over the short to medium term. As we noted earlier, changes in the age distribution of the population can have important short run effects and this will certainly be the case in the next five years. Over this period, the relative decline in the numbers reaching retirement age and the increase in those of school leaving age means that the population of working age will increase by some 750,000 by 1986[7].

In mid 1981, on the basis of the declining activity rates and population projections, the Department of Employment projected an increase in the labour force of around 700,000 by 1986. This projection was based on the assumption that unemployment would peak in 1982 and thereafter decline to around two million in 1986. It was also assumed that activity rates for married women aged 35-54 would rise until 1986 — by between two and five percentage points for the different age groups. But on the assumption that births would rise by 20 per cent between 1979 and 1986, the activity rates for married women aged between 25 and 34 were projected to fall by some three percentage points. In terms of numbers this increase in the birth rate could be expected to reduce the female labour force by about 100,000

The results of these projections are given in Table 5, and it is worth noting that they are sensitive to the underlying assumptions about the level of unemployment and activity rates. If unemployment in 1986 is below the two million central assumption, for example at 1.5 million instead, the labour force will increase by 1 million; whereas if it remain 2.5 million, the labour force will only increase by 500,000. has already been noted that present unemployment is highe than projected and activity rates will probably have already responded to an unknown extent. These total estimates car also be disaggregated to show regional trends, and in some cases, East Anglia and the South West for example, the increases in the labour force may be substantially higher th the national average[8].

Table 5. Future labour force

	1979 % GB total	1986 % GB total	1979-1986 increase % change
Males	60.6	60.1	1.6
Females	39.4	39.9	3.8
Married females	25.9	25.6	1.0
Non-married females	13.4	14.3	9.1
All persons	100.0	100.0	2.5
Base (=100%) (000's)	26,028	26,672	644

Source: Labour Force Outlook to 1986, Employment Gazette, Apr 1981, Table 5.1.

As we noted at the beginning of this section, employment projections are based on a range of specified assumptions. S far, we have discussed the future implications of demograp and social change and the difficulties and uncertainties involved. In the short to medium term, changes in global economic trends and internal economic policy may also ha considerable impact. Even if such trends were favourable it would take some time for the economy to 'pick up', and unemployment would remain well above late 1970s levels the mid 1980s. However, in the medium to longer term, it perhaps the possible effects of technological change which have generated the most controversy in recent years. We m on now to discuss some of these issues.

Technological change and employment trends

So far we have described a number of long term trends in t composition of the labour force and the nature and volume employment, and we have discussed some short term projections for the future. We turn briefly now to consider the implications of what many commentators believe to be an unprecedented rate of technological change.

The speed of technological change since the first computer was built 30 years ago has certainly been dramatic, and in many respects is aptly described as a revolution. Robert Noyce, chairman of the Intel Corporation vividly summed up the essential elements of this revolution when he noted that:

"Today's micro computer. . . has more computing capacity than the first large electronic computers. It is 20 times faster, has a larger memory, is thousands of times more reliable, consumes the power of a light bulb rather than that of a locomotive, occupies 1/30,000 of the volume and costs 1/10,000 as much.' much."[9]

'New technology' incorporates a wide range of 'applications' centred on the cheapness and flexibility of the micro processor or 'chip'. The most far reaching of these are the developments included under the heading 'Information Technology' for it has been estimated that as many as 65 per cent of the labour force now work in what may be broadly defined as information occupations[10]. The list of over 200 uses drawn up in the Department of Industry booklet 'Microelectronics — The New Technology' clearly demonstrates the ubiquitous nature of these and other developments[11]. The impact will be widespread, but the nature and magnitude is more problematic.

The public debate about new technology has focussed primarily on the overall impact on jobs. There are those who believe that new jobs will be created and that the new technology will bring prosperity for all, whilst others claim it can only lead to mass unemployment. But the **total** quantifiable impact is unpredictable. To date there has been both job loss (as at the Volvo factory where the introduction of robots reduced the number of operators each shift from 50 to 10)[12], and job creation (in both the production of the hardware and software of the technology itself and in the production of new products). Both the creation and destruction of jobs will happen directly and indirectly (when for example new technology in one sector affects the competitiveness and/or profitability of another sector) and it will be impossible to identify all such changes. In addition, the effects of technology are presently largely overshadowed by the effects of a severe recession.

It is, however, predictable that many jobs in specific sectors

will be and are being lost. In manufacturing, microelectron
will affect both the production process itself and the natur
the products — changes which will affect employment.
Automation of production processes has already led to
significant reductions in the workforce in various industrie
For example, as a result of the introduction of new
technologies, the workforce of the National Cash Register
Company fell from 37,000 in 1970 to 18,000 in 1975[13].
Similarly, a new textile mill opened in Manchester by
Carrington Viyella, replaced three former plants and emplc
95 people as opposed to 435 in the old plants[14]. Microelectronics will also lead to a reduction in the number of
components in certain products such as televisions and sew
machines. This will also mean job loss for those manufactu
and assembling the components, as well as those moving,
storing and servicing machine parts. Such changes were
influential in the loss of more than 2,000 jobs at Thorn
Electrical Industries in Bradford[15].

If UK manufacturing industry experiences an increased
demand for its products in the future, there are therefore
those who believe it to be quite possible that it will be 'job
growth' which occurs[16]. There are, however, others who
believe that microelectronics will stimulate the production
whole range of new products and create totally new jobs,
and that the new technology might also stimulate higher
productivity across a range of industries through a multipli
effect[17]. However, such a scenario depends crucially on the
investment of any additional income in employment
generating activities. It is also questionable, whether suffici
new jobs will be generated in manufacturing alone to matc
the present scale of unemployment. Furthermore, the effec
of new technologies will not be confined to the manufactu
sector.

The office sector is another area around which there is som
consensus that information technology in particular will ca
loss of jobs, although estimates vary considerably ranging fi
a 2 per cent decline, to losses of the order of 30 per cent b
the mid 1980s.[18] Similarly, new technologies are expected
be widely applied in sales and distribution, banking and
insurance, education, health and welfare services and post a
telecommunications[19]. This will bring about considerable
changes in employment. On the basis of available evidence
would be fair to say that in the short term (and clearly not
solely related to the introduction of new technology) more
are being lost than are being gained. In addition it would se

that many of the new jobs require new skills. Shortages are therefore developing in parallel with the dislocation of workers with obsolete skills.

The Manpower Service Commission (MSC), for example, recently identified skill shortages in electronics, engineering and software (programme) design.[20] New jobs are being created in connection with data processing, systems analysis and research and development, positions which do not presently match the skills available amongst that section of the labour force most at risk of losing employment. In particular this situation presents special problems for older workers who may find it difficult to adapt to the demands for flexibility and retraining thrown up by microelectronics, for many young workers who lack training and for women, who are characteristically under-represented on many training courses.

Older workers. As we have seen, the activity rates for men and women in the older age groups have declined sharply in recent years and they may be expected to continue to do so, especially with an increasing emphasis on early retirement. But as we discuss in Part 3, retirement, like unemployment, can have severe financial and social consequences for the individuals involved and for their families, particularly if it is involuntary[21]. There is a widespread, though unproven, assumption that older workers will inevitably be unable to cope with today's pace of change. Retraining for this age group is therefore insignificant in relation to all training provisions and will continue to be so in the context of massive youth unemployment. Both many older workers themselves, and the public at large, generally accept the view that the older worker should make way for the young though the evidence suggests that such replacement is not happening to the extent many had hoped for[22].

Younger workers. We have already seen that today's unemployment is disproportionately affecting younger workers. A recent estimate by the Manpower Services Commission suggests that 68 per cent of under 18 year olds leaving full time education in 1983 will be unable to find work and the figure is likely to remain at this sort of level for some time to come[23].

Though youth unemployment and overall levels of unemployment are closely associated the former rises at a much faster rate — as indeed it has in recent years[24]. The possible explanations for this relationship — for example, recruitment policies, relative pay levels, demographic factors, occupational

segregation — are presently the subjects of debate but it is
possibility that demand for young workers may be changir
permanently which we address here.

It has been argued that the retail and service sectors will
provide new jobs for young workers as jobs are lost in the
manufacturing sector. However, young people, and especia
girls, are already over represented in retail distribution
industries and since 1966 employment in retailing has beei
declining.

Without a restructuring of education and training the adve
of new technologies can only exacerbate this situation, ye
Britain is apparently providing less education and training
16-18 year olds than any other OECD country[25].

The major 'training' provision for young people at the
moment is the Youth Opportunities Programme (YOP) wr
though available to young people up to 24 focusses primar
on school leavers. During the year 1980/81 one in three sc
leavers entered this programme which offers a range of
placements. The vast majority of projects, however, provic
work experience rather than training[26]. This scheme has a
number of problems, but in the context of this discussion
there are perhaps two critical issues. Firstly the extent of
training in YOP is very limited and secondly a rapidly
declining number of 'trainees' manage to obtain a job afte
leaving — only 30 per cent on average at the end of 1981.'

There has recently been a series of reports on training
provision culminating in the publication of a White Paper
December 1981. 'A New Training Initiative' sets out the
Government's plans for a new training scheme for 16 year
to start in September 1982 with some provisions for older
workers[28]. Unfortunately the financial burden which trair
implies for many families has been relatively neglected in
White Paper, an issue we return to in Part 3.

Women workers. The position of women in the labour ma
may also be disproportionately affected in the future by t
advent of new technologies. They are already disadvantage
the labour market. Studies have repeatedly identified a m
separation of women's occupations and men's, and despit
major changes in the labour force and employment descri
earlier, and the recent implementation of equal opportuni
legislation, this situation has changed very little. Today
around 27 per cent of all women work in occupations in v
they outnumber men by nine to one, and 58 per cent of r
work in occupations where they similarly outnumber

women[29]. There is also a clear separation **within** particular occupations between different grades, with women typically filling the lower status posts.

One writer has recently illustrated the continuation of such separation, using an 'index of occupational segregation' — that is, the extent to which women are over- or under-represented in particular areas[30]. Some examples are given in Table 6. If men and women were equally represented the index would be one, the higher the figure the greater the concentration of women. As is clearly seen women are **under**-represented in higher professional and managerial posts, and in engineering and technology for example, though the position in the latter posts has improved. They are **over**-represented in catering, cleaning, clerical and health and welfare professions — the very jobs which many commentators argue will be most dramatically transformed by the rapid spread of micro-electronics.

Table 6. Under- and over-representation of women in selected occupational groups 1973-79

Degree of under- or over-representation in each group in relation to the female proportion of the total labour force

	1973	1977	1979
Professional and related supporting management and administration	0.38	0.41	0.54
Professional and related in education, welfare and health	1.67	1.62	1.62
Professional and related in science, engineering and technology	0.13	0.15	0.23
Managerial	0.51	0.49	0.54
Clerical and related	1.94	1.91	1.87
Selling	1.54	1.47	1.54
Catering, cleaning, hairdressing	2.16	2.09	2.10
Processing, making, repairing and related (excluding metal and electrical)	0.92	0.85	0.87
Painting, repetitive assembling, product inspecting, packaging and related	1.20	1.21	1.18
Transport operating, materials moving and storing and related	0.11	0.10	0.13

Source: Employment Gazette, December 1981, p 525

Note: If men and women were equally represented the index would be one. The higher the figure the greater the concentration of women.

The implications for women's employment are not, howeve restricted to the office and service sectors — women's employment in manufacturing is also threatened. It is predominantly the unskilled and semi skilled tasks in manufacturing which are most susceptible to automation, those sectors where as Table 6 shows, women are again ove represented. In the textile industry, for example 75 per cer of the workforce is female and, as the example of the Carrington Viyella factory in Manchester illustrated, this industry has increasingly introduced automated techniques Similarly, the redundancies at the Thorn factory in Bradfo involved a large number of women workers, some 200 of whom were retrained for clerical work. However, the local ASTMS office estimated that many clerical, secretarial and administrative jobs would disappear from the city between 1979 and 1983[31].

The table suggests that segregation did appear to decline a little in the mid 1970s, but any gains seem to have been alr completely reversed by 1979. Though this is partly the res of the recession, in the future the introduction of new technologies may speed up this reversal unless there is a considerable expansion of training and positive encourager to women to join more advanced courses.

Women are, however, considerably under-represented on s training courses. In 1978/79 for example, they made up or per cent of trainees on science and technology courses but per cent of those on clerical and commercial courses — a complete reversal[32]. There is some evidence to suggest tha women are more involved than men in training for basic de skills. These are related to lower level non professional computer related work suggesting a continuation of traditi patterns of segregation[33].

New technologies: the nature of work and other issues

New technologies may have other far reaching effects on t nature of employment in the future but, as with any exerc concerned to predict future trends, the longer the time sca the less certain the predictions can be. This is undoubtedly case in relation to new technologies. However, because the effects could be important for the relationship between w and the family some mention should be made of these issu tentative though these comments will be.

Recent changes in patterns of work have already been described. As more women have entered the labour marke

44

there has been a slow but perceptible reduction in the differences between men's and women's pattern of work. (Although it could justifiably be claimed that to date it is women who have moved closer towards men's pattern of work and that they have retained the major responsibilities for the home and child care.) Increasing provision of paternity leave, realistic early retirement options, sabbaticals and other trends may in the future facilitate a more equal distribution of home/work responsibilities. It is possible that new technologies could also contribute by allowing more flexible working time and work closer to, or indeed in, the home.

In relation to homeworking in particular, developments in telecommunications have opened up the possibility for office jobs to be based in the home and dispersed geographically[34]. Though little progress has so far occurred in this area in the UK, developments elsewhere suggest that as commuting costs escalate this may become a more attractive proposition. Any significant increase in home-working, however, raises a host of complex issues at an individual, company and societal level. Potentially for example, the rating system, property prices, the tax system and pension rights might all be affected[35].

It would be impossible to predict what the combined effects of such influences might be but developments in homeworking could have advantages for parents with family responsibilities, for handicapped or other people who would be unwilling or unable to travel to work and could help to alleviate regional unemployment. One American bank, for example, already employs young mothers, handicapped and retired people as home word processing clerks[36]. Though present initiatives involve mostly low grade jobs the potential is great. However, working from home is not without its disadvantages. The social component of the work environment would be lost completely, and many costs would be transferred to the worker — heating, lighting and so on.

One way in which many of the disadvantages of homeworking for the employee could be avoided, whilst ensuring the advantages of decentralisation, is through the development of Neighbourhood Work Centres. Such centres are established by several companies jointly renting or purchasing space in buildings close to residential areas. Though there have again been few examples of such developments so far in this country they certainly represent a longer term option, and the French government is currently undertaking a major study on their viability[37]. In a recent series of interviews with eight senior planners, technologists and sociologists in this country it was clear that they felt such developments to be feasible,

but not until after 1990[38]. In the same report, however, it
also suggested that these 'experts' felt such developments
would favour women with professional qualifications in
particular — a group who presently represent only a very s
proportion of all women workers.

A further note of caution is sounded by those who sugges
that rather than be widely dispersed, the benefits of new
technologies, and the jobs they generate, will be geograph
concentrated. Though there is very little information abou
present trends in this area, it is certainly the case that 'Hi
Tech' industries today are mainly growing in the South Ea
in the Bristol area and around Cambridge.

Similarly an Equal Opportunities Commission (EOC) repo
the possible effects of new technology on women's work
found that none of the organisations surveyed planned to
the new technologies to make more part time work availal
and roughly equal numbers of the respondants felt that th
new technologies would make it easier or more difficult tc
return to work following absence due, for example, to fan
commitments such as child rearing[39]. Furthermore, the
interim report of a study of the impact of technological
change on women's work in West Yorkshire, concluded th
there was little evidence of any increase in part-time work
homework[40]. Given the initial expense of many of the ne
automated systems there may also be pressure to get
maximum return on capital expenditure which may ultim.
mean pressure to extend hours of operation into shift wor
and other unsocial hours of work. For example, at the lar
textile plant in Manchester mentioned earlier, the highly
capital intensive equipment 'will be operated seven days a
week, 24 hours a day, using a complex five shift system'.[4]

Part 3

Employment trends and the family

In this section of the paper we consider the links between the trends in employment which we have described and 'the family'. We consider the issues from two perspectives. Firstly, how do family membership and responsibilities affect an individual's ability to work outside the home, or the hours or type of work that can or will be undertaken and how does this vary for different family members Secondly, we discuss how people's employment experiences affect their family lives, drawing a distinction between the economic and social consequences.

Section A : Labour supply and the life cycle of family responsibilities

In earlier sections we described recent trends and possible future trends in the level and structure of employment and in working patterns. In this section we focus on the employment profiles of individuals as they relate to family status, and attempt to explain why these profiles differ. We note too the impact of a number of demographic trends which are affecting the nature of family responsibilities over the life cycle, and the whole notion of 'family'.

Men and women

For men the typical employment profile is to enter the labour force at the end of full time schooling or training and to participate full time until retirement. Only a very small proportion of men work part time and they are most likely to do so as a prelude to retirement. For women, on the other hand, the employment profile is quite different.

Figure 5 shows a number of typical employment 'profiles'; for men, married women and unmarried women, based on cross sectional data for 1979[1]. It shows clearly the lower level of labour force participation of women in the 25-34 age group, and also suggests that the employment behaviour of non married women is more like that of men than their married

counterparts although it is still interestingly different from
Why does the employment profile of married women
presented here differ so substantially from that of men? It
clearly the case — and research evidence supports this — th
large part of the explanation of women's employment
behaviour relates to their responsibility for caring for
children[2].

Figure 5. Activity rates Great Britain

Percentage economically active

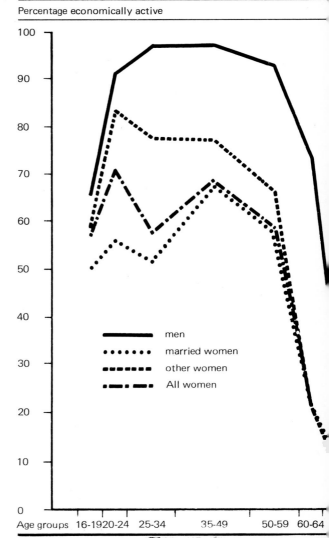

Source: Published and unpublished data from the 1979 Labour Fo
Survey, OPCS, HMSO, 1982

Children

The presence of children affects the likelihood that a woman will work outside the home, whether or not she works 'part time' (or more generally the hours that she can work) and even the type of work she feels able to undertake. Mothers are far less likely to be working than women without children. In 1979 69 per cent of women without dependent children were working, compared with only 52 per cent of those with dependent children. And when mothers do work they are far more likely than other women to be working part time. Again in 1979, 70 per cent of working mothers were working part time compared with only 26 per cent of working women without dependent children[3].

Both the **number** of children for whom a woman is responsible and their ages affect her participation. Mothers with two children are just as likely to work as those with one child but are more likely to work part time. On the other hand mothers with three or more children are less likely to be working at all. But overall, it is the age of the youngest child, and particularly the presence of a child under five, which is the main determinant of whether or not women work outside the home, and whether or not they work full time. In 1979 only 28 per cent of women whose youngest child was under five were working; three-quarters of these mothers worked part time. In contrast 72 per cent of women whose youngest child was aged 10 or over were working, of whom only 63 per cent were part time[4].

It is still very rare, then, for mothers with pre-school children to work full time — indeed only 6 per cent of such mothers do so. And it is clear that part time work is an important way in which women with children combine work and family responsibilities. Indeed in the 1965 national survey of women's employment, two thirds of women who were working part time gave their responsibilities for children as the reason for doing so[5]. In addition it affected the hours at which they worked:

"A third only worked during school hours and 13 per cent gave up paid work during school holidays. A further 6.5 per cent of employed mothers responsible for the children worked evenings, early mornings or overnight; times when father could be home. In contrast, among employed women without children only 1.5 per cent confined their paid employment to those times."[6]

This survey is obviously very dated now, and more up to d
information will become available from the 'Women and
Employment' survey[7]. But it does highlight the importanc
child care facilities in enabling women to work, or to work
hours they would prefer. This has been confirmed by sever
surveys over a long period. In 1974 for example a national
survey showed that day care facilities were wanted for twi
many children as currently used them[8]. More recently a
national survey of women who had babies in 1979 showed
that better and more extensive child care facilities for wor
women ranked far above any other change that women wc
like to see to enable them to stay at work during their
childbearing and childrearing years[9].

But it has also recently been suggested that the **type** of wo
which women undertake is related to their home
responsibilities. A study of women factory workers, for
example, noted that 'employment has to be fitted in with
their household duties and child care arrangements which
and their families regard as unquestionably their responsib
Factory work is often seen as the only job possible in the
circumstances, and entered into more from necessity than
choice'[10].

Fathers

Whereas the impact of children on their mothers' employn
has been subjected to much scrutiny far less than been wri
about the situation of fathers. Yet as Moss noted in 1977,

"In 1971 in Britain there were three million fathers with a
child under five and a further 2.1 millions with a younger
of primary school age."[11]

Today married men with dependent children account for
per cent of the male labour force, and on this basis there a
some 6.8 million fathers working or seeking work. Activity
rates among married men tend to be higher than among nc
married men, and also to be higher among married men wi
dependent children than among those without[12]. And 'In
contrast to the pattern among mothers the proportion of
fathers in work did not vary with the age of their youngest
child. Nor did it vary with the number of dependent childr
in the family . . .'[13]. Also, whereas women with children te
to work fewer hours, the majority of fathers work full tim
and fathers of large families, who tend to have lower hour
earnings, work longer hours on average than fathers in sma
families[14]. Equally, a number of studies suggest that paid

time is most common among younger married men, especially those with dependent children, whose financial commitments are often high: one study showed that married men under thirty with children worked four times as much paid overtime as similarly aged childless husbands[15]. Similarly, men with children are more likely to work shifts.

The picture presented above is, however, inadequate in at least three important ways. First it fails to reflect the impact of children on their mothers' employment opportunities **over time**.[16] The vast majority of women give up work at the birth of their first child. When they return to work the majority of mothers work part time. But part time working is often confined to lower grade posts, is consequently often low paid, and also relatively insecure. Part timers are often excluded from fringe benefits, and are seldom properly integrated into promotion or seniority structures[17]. Thus in the longer term, as we discuss later, periods of part time working to accommodate family responsibilities may adversely affect women's earnings and the quality of job opportunities open to them. The same may hold for breaks in employment per se, the effect of which is now being studied[18].

Secondly — a point to which we return — such a snapshot, cross sectional picture shows different groups — or cohorts — of women at different stages in their family cycle. It does not adequately show the employment profile of the **same** group of women as they grow older. Working women of 55 and 60 are likely to have different employment histories to groups of younger women now entering the labour market. We return to discuss this in the context of the changing relationship between employment and the family.

The third major inadequacy of the picture presented so far is that it is static in its view of family responsibilities in the light of changing family patterns, and it is to this that we now turn.

Changing Family Patterns

While the focus of most discussions has been the impact of children on their parents' employment behaviour, there is a growing awareness of the implications of the rapid ageing of the elderly population. The population over retirement age has increased by nearly 30 per cent over the last twenty years, and although the total number of people over retirement age is now projected not to rise by the end of the century, there will be substantial changes in the age structure within the elderly population.

By the end of the century the number of people aged 75 a
over is expected to increase by about one-fifth, and the
number aged 85 and over by no less than one-half. In con
the number of people between retirement age and 75 will
decrease by 11 per cent over the same period[19].

As people become older it is more likely that they will be
frail, and be in need of care from their families, and from
others. When this is combined with a renewed emphasis o
'community care' policies (which in reality often means
family care), it is clear that the situation of workers carin
elderly dependants is likely to loom large over the next
decade[20].

The extent of these responsibilities is difficult to gauge
because few studies have focussed on the situation of 'car
But, as with children, the majority of the burden falls on
women[21]. Hunt's 1965 survey of women's employment
showed that one working woman in ten and one non wor
woman in eight was responsible for the care of at least on
elderly or infirm person[22]. Her study also showed that or
five housewives aged between 35 and 49 years, had a disa
person or someone aged over 65 in the household. Amon
those aged between 50 and 64 this was true of one in fou

Since that time the number of very elderly people has
increased considerably and very recently, a small scale stu
the North East found that there were more 'carers' of
handicapped or elderly dependants than there were moth
children under 16[24].

Mirroring the situation with children, responsibility for e
or infirm dependants can affect whether or not someone
able to work outside the home at all, or it can affect hou
worked, or their 'choice' of employment. The 1965 surve
showed that women responsible for the care of elderly or
infirm persons were less likely to be working than others,
if they were working they were less likely to be working
time[25]. One in six part time workers with these responsib
said she was compelled to work part time because of her
responsibilities. And over a fifth of all working women w
these responsibilities said that their employment was affe
in some way — mainly by being forced to take time off w
Hunt's survey of elderly people showed that among wom
who gave up work between the ages of 40 and 59, the ne
look after people other than their husbands comes secon
to ill health as a reason for giving up work[26]. Yet the
employment implications of these responsibilities are sel
recognised, and the fact that women (and men) may be

involved in a **sequence** of caring — for children, elderly relatives and frail, elderly spouses — has yet to be appreciated[27].

The ageing of the population is just one of the significant trends that are affecting the nature of family responsibilities: the other major trends are those in marriage breakdown and remarriage. Today one in three 'new' marriages is likely to end in divorce[28]. In addition some couples separate but do not subsequently divorce, or do so only after a lengthy period. In either case the effects of disharmony at home may well spill over into working life, and indeed we have already noted that widowed, divorced and separated men suffer higher rates of unemployment than their married counterparts[29].

But the major impact of divorce and separation in this context is in the increasing number of one parent families, the majority of which are headed by women. Today one in eight children is being brought up in a one parent family and nearly one million lone parents have the care of one and a half million children. Even this, however, understates the importance of lone parenthood, and we have estimated elsewhere that between one in five and one in six children born today will see their parents divorce during their childhood.

Lone mothers are slightly less likely to be working than other mothers — 46 per cent compared with 52 per cent[30]. And whereas other mothers have been increasingly likely to work during the 1970s lone mothers have become less likely to do so[31]. But there are important differences within the lone mother group — with divorced and widowed mothers more likely to be working, and single and separated mothers less likely to be so than other mothers[32]. When they do work, lone mothers are **more** likely to work full time than their married counterparts, which is in some ways paradoxical given their single handed responsibility for child care.

The decision of a lone mother to work or not to work, and if to work on what basis to do so, must be a very difficult one, given both the complexity of the income support system in its interaction with earnings, and the ambiguity of attitudes surrounding mothers working. These issues are discussed in some detail elsewhere[33], but it is worth noting two points here. First, when they do work, lone mothers are less likely to be in poverty than when they do not[34], and second, that non-financial reasons for working are often cited by lone mothers whose financial return from working may be small. Indeed the author of a study of lone mothers receiving Family Income Supplement (FIS) commented that 'The importance for lone

mothers of this social dimension of work should not go
unnoticed since it is clearly a main contributory factor in
very positive attitude towards employment'[35].

Lone fathers are far more likely to work than lone mothe
reflecting their potentially higher earnings, and lone fathe
working hours are similar to those of fathers in two paren
families. But a pioneering study of motherless families cle
showed the impact of responsibility for young children or
their fathers' working patterns. Such fathers worked less
overtime, were less able to work at weekends, and could r
undertake jobs which involved travel from home[36].

Currently we know too little about the duration of lone
parenthood, but for some parents and children it will be a
short transitional phase before remarriage brings about a
reconstituted, family. Again, the effect that these changes
on the employment behaviour of parents is uncharted, bu
certainly become more important as it affects more and n
families. The other major change in family patterns is the
decline in family size, and we discuss this in the context c
way the relationship between employment and the family
been changing.

Changing relationships between work and the family

We have noted the increased number of women in the lat
force, and that the major part of this increase is due to th
changed behaviour of married women. Since the war, the
differential in economic activity between married and oth
women has diminished, although it is still true that marrie
women remain less likely to work than single women. Bu
out of ten married women will have children at some tim
their lives, and this marital status differential is more
appropriately viewed as an effect of childbearing[37]. Thus

"The rise of the working wife in post war Britain has thus
largely also been the rise of the working mother. Before t
war, mothers of dependent children participated in the la
force very rarely. Their overall participation must be pres
to be lower than the 12 per cent of all wives under 60. By
late 1970s the non working mother was in a minority, roi
half of all dependent children had a working mother, and
two fifths of the female workforce were working mothers

Indeed it seems that the fastest **increases** in participation
1970s were for women with young children.

The cross sectional picture presented previously, therefore encapsulates two distinct phenomena — the impact of family responsibilities over the life cycle, and the changing behaviour of different cohorts of women. Figure 6 illustrates some aspects of these changes. It shows that successive cohorts of women have had higher levels of labour force participation and that the fall in activity during the childbearing period has been compressed into a shorter period of time. This partly reflects the fact that families are smaller today, but also that children may be 'spaced' through the use of contraception. It is also the case the women are less likely than previously to give up work on marriage, but still tend to do so at the birth of their first

Figure 6. Actual and projected female employee rates 1950-74, 1975-2009

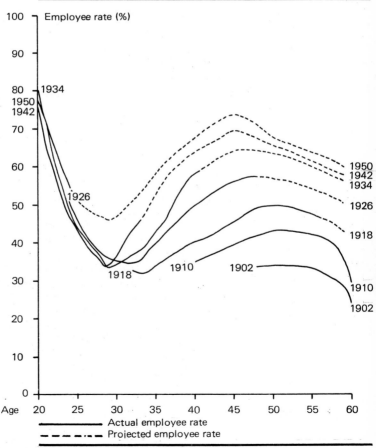

Source: H Joshi & S Owen 1981 Chart 1.3 Reference[2]
Note: Projections are based on assumptions specified in the source.

child. But more women are returning to work within a yea
their children's birth. Whereas the 1971 Census showed tha
only 9 per cent of mothers of babies aged under one year w
economically active, the national survey in 1979 showed th
nearly one quarter were economically active by the time th
babies were eight months old[39]. Similarly Dunnell's study
family formation showed a slight increase in the proportio
mothers who returned to work before the birth of their se
child[40].

Much of the change in women's levels of economic activity
taken place in the 1970s during which time women's
participation rates increased from 55 per cent to 61 per ce
and those of mothers from 41 per cent to 52 per cent[41].

But what explains these changes?

At one level the explanation is simple, and reflects the gro
of part time employment opportunities. In 1971 33 per ce
of all women were working full time and a further 22 per c
part time. By 1979 34 per cent were working full time and
further 26 per cent part time. For mothers the increase is r
dramatic: 15 per cent were working full time in 1971 and
per cent in 1979. But whereas a further 26 per cent were
working part time in 1971 this had risen to 36 per cent by
1979[42]. Thus at a macro level all the increase in the
employment of women with dependent children in the 197
is attributable to the increase in part time work.

But this itself begs the question of why part time job
opportunities increased; Can their expansion be most
adequately explained by factors on the 'demand' side, or b
those on the 'supply' side?

On the demand side any decrease in hours supplied by oth
groups of workers may increase the willingness of employe
to offer employment on terms to suit wives and mothers.
Greenhalgh, for example, notes that for the period 1951-1
the absolute increase in labour supply by wives almost exa
offset reductions in labour supply from men and single
women, which arose both from a decrease in average week
hours and from a shortening of the average length of worki
life[43]. Interestingly, one in eight of the women in Hunt's 1
survey who had returned to work after a break said that at
least part of the reason they had done so was that they had
been 'asked to help out'[44]. This may also have been a fact
during the 1970s when there was a reduction in the averag
working week.

The changes we have documented must, however, also reflect a greater willingness to undertake work outside the home than previously. Why should this be? At the outset it is important to recognise that the reasons why more mothers work and whether they should do so are questions about which there are sincere and deeply held differences of opinion. It is not possible to give definitive answers to these questions: there may be a variety of reasons why women as a whole, or an individual woman, seeks paid employment, or increases or reduces her hours of work. Also, since the majority of women now work between marriage and the birth of their first child, but then leave work, what we are in fact trying to explain is why they return to work earlier than previously, and in greater numbers.

On this, a national survey of mothers of new babies conducted in 1979 provides some valuable insights. The survey showed that mothers at opposite ends of the occupational scale were more likely than others to be back in work shortly after the birth of their babies. Forty one per cent of women in occupational grades I and II were in work after the birth as were 52 per cent of unskilled women, and these proportions were about twice as great as for other occupational groups. Although the study did not collect direct information on why women returned to work, the author, W W Daniel, found it 'Tempting to speculate that qualified women returned because of the relatively high rewards of their jobs, while the unskilled were more likely to return out of financial necessity'[45]. If this is so then both a woman's own potential earnings and those of her husband are important determinants of her employment patterns.

Following this reasoning the study conducted for the Royal Commission on the Distribution of Income and Wealth (RCDIW) noted that both these variables have been changing:

"Between the war and 1973 women's and men's real wages roughly doubled. These changes would predict an increase in participation of about 10 percentage points — compared with the increase of 30 points which actually occurred for women under 60. Between April 1973 and April 1977 women's gross real wages increased by about 10 per cent while men's real wages fell by nearly as much. This of itself would predict an increase in participation of over 3 percentage points, compared with an actual increase of 5 percentage points".[46]

Women's potential earnings were also affected by the passage of the Equal Pay Act in 1975, after which their earnings rose in relation to those of men from 67.4 per cent in 1974 to 75.5 per cent in 1977[47].

57

But while increases in their own potential earnings are like
to have been the most important factor in increasing wom
participation, we should not ignore the relative decline in
men's wages referred to above. Equally the increase in wor
by mothers may also be related to the increased tax burde
families with children. Field, for example, notes that

"Over the period from 1964/5 to 1979/80 the tax burden c
single person on average earnings increased by 29 percenta
points while for a married couple with two children the
increase was in the order of 137 percentage points"[48].

More recently, Piachaud has noted that a decline in the re
value of child support between 1950 and 1981 has been o
by the increase in two earner families[49]. In general familie
where the wife works, are, if her earnings are excluded, pc
than other families[50]. In essence:

". . . the extra wage often does no more than bring the join
household income up to an acceptable level in compensati
for the low wages of one partner"[51].

Further it has been noted by the Central Policy Review S
(CPRS) that there would be three or four times as many
families in poverty — normally defined as a level of incom
below 140 per cent of their supplementary benefit entitle
— were it not for the wife's earnings[52].

Financial reasons are, then, particularly for some groups,
important part of work motivation. In Hunt's survey, for
example, two thirds of manual workers' wives cited 'need
the money' in contrast to just over half of non manual
workers' wives[53]. But such factors do not offer a total
explanation of the increase in women's employment, and
non financial benefits of working for women should not b
ignored. Again Hunt's survey, though dated, is instructive
found that reasons such as 'company, interest and to avoi
boredom' were more likely to be cited than financial reas
by women in higher social classes, but also that these reas
were nearly twice as likely to be cited by women in house
households containing children, than by those in househo
where there were adults only[54]. More recently Dunnell's s
found that of those who returned to work between their
and second babies an increasing proportion in the most re
cohorts reported that they did so 'because they liked it'[55]

Equally, studies of those caring for elderly or handicappe
relatives have shown that a job may act as a vital lifeline,
counteract the isolation of their caring role[56]. However,

financial problems (handwritten annotation)

58

the results of the current 'Women and Employment' survey become available, it is difficult to know how far these non financial aspects of work motivation have changed.

Neither is it possible, at this stage, to assess adequately how far other changes have affected the willingness or ability of women to work. But there are two issues worthy of note: the first is the impact of divorce on women's orientation to employment and the second is the impact of men's unemployment on their wives' labour market participation.

Currently there is much debate about the financial arrangements between spouses after divorce, and particularly about the payment of maintenance to former wives[57]. Proposals recently put forward would, if implemented, make it more likely that maintenance payments would be awarded for a limited period after which a woman would be expected to support herself through her own earnings. Were the law to be changed in this way, it could well affect the importance which women would attach to maintaining their own careers, and their earnings potential. But even without such a change in the law, it is open to question whether the rapid increase in divorce rates over the last twenty years has in fact already altered women's views about the need for a source of income independent of their husband's earnings.

Uncertainty about income also arises from increasing levels of unemployment. How far does the threat of unemployment act as an incentive to families to spread the risk by relying on more than one wage earner? And how far do women, with husbands who become unemployed, take up work to raise the family's income? It is not possible to answer the first of these questions, but new data from the cohort studies of the unemployed will enable us to begin to answer the latter. It is known that unemployed men are, contrary to expectations, **less** likely to have working wives than their employed counterparts[58]. But this static picture does not as it stands allow us to draw conclusions about the effects of men's unemployment on the labour force behaviour of their wives, or indeed of other members of their families. We need to know whether wives **change** their employment status once their husbands become unemployed. Both the cohort studies confirm the conclusions of earlier research that, in the short term at least, there is little effect. In particular 'it seems fairly safe to conclude that if unemployment of the family head does stimulate increased labour force participation by the wife or other family members, the effect is small'[59]. But although the overriding result is one of little effect,' . . . it cannot be concluded that their husbands' unemployment had no effect on the labour market status of the women. The crucial point to remember is that a high proportion of the men had had previous spells of registered unemployment and it is possible that the wives had responded to that situation prior to the period of unemployment being considered by this study'[60]. On the other hand, unemployment and employment opportunities are heavily concentrated geographically and t may be a more important part of the explanation of the low participation and higher unemployment of wives of unemployed men. This issue, however, does highlight the extent to which husbands' and wives' employment are interdependent, and it is to the decision making process with the family that we now turn our attention.

Decision making within the family

In many cases, and on the assumption that families normally depend only on one breadwinner, the 'family' is taken as th 'unit' of labour supply. In other words, very little attention has been paid to decisions **within** the family about who sho work or the timing or extent of that work. It is possible on basis of the employment profiles described earlier to surmis that traditionally parents have combined their parental and work responsibilities by a 'sexual division of labour', with father working outside the home and mother working with it, doing the housework and caring for the children. Some argue that such a rigid division between parental roles is breaking down, and that the stereotype of men's and wome roles in childcare and domestic work is weakening. But the a very real debate about just how far any such change has gone, and there is no doubt that rigid role relationships stil exist in many households. Equally, while it is possible to undertake studies which measure changes in wives' employment in response to changes in husbands' income or employment status, there has been very little work done or the actual processes of decision making within the family.

A valuable exception to this is the work of Marsh on the question of shiftwork[61]. His study gives some fascinating insights into 'the domestic climate in which the decision fc wife to work shifts would be taken'[62]. In some families thi may be a source of some dispute. In 29 per cent of the cou surveyed, the wife strongly disagreed and the husband stro agreed with the statement 'a woman's place is in the home' and in 11 per cent the disharmony was reversed. However, while 13 years previously Hunt's survey had suggested that some 14 per cent of women were 'working in the teeth of husband's disapproval' Marsh's survey showed only 2 per c of husbands taking this view[63]. He notes, however, that his sample was of women in inner city areas where 'the pressing need of many couples to earn more together to maintain a reasonable standard of living overrides a husband's reservations about the wisdom of "allowing" his wife to work'.

Decisions within the family take place within the context of more general social values and attitudes. It is evident that social attitudes surrounding the way in which husbands and wives, mothers and fathers choose to organise their work and family lives are in a state of flux. But in many ways, the choices available to individuals, especially those with family responsibilities, are limited by such things as the availability of substitute child care, or the flexibility of working hours. Thus we need a far greater appreciation of the importance of public policies as a framework within which individuals may choose how to combine their various responsibilities.

Having discussed ways in which changing family obligations over the life cycle and changing family patterns affect family members' ability to participate in the labour market, we now turn the issue on its head and discuss the effects of employment and unemployment on families.

Section B: Employment trends: economic and social consequences for families

In the preceeding section we have discussed how family membership and responsibilities affect an individual's ability to work outside the home, the hours and/or type of work that can and/or will be undertaken, and how this varies for different family members. These decisions will have a range of both positive and negative consequences for the families involved. In this section therefore, we look at some of these consequences. For simplicity we have drawn a rather arbitrary distinction between the economic and social consequences but we would of course acknowledge the close relationship between these.

Economic consequences

The links between economic well being and paid employment are direct and obvious: employment incomes are the largest component of personal income; much of the social security system during and after working life is linked to employment status and earnings; and for a growing number of people private pensions and other benefits are also linked to employment.

Family incomes and employment

Earnings from employment are the major income source fo[r]
96 per cent of all two parent families[1]. In the majority of
these families it is the man's earnings which dominate, but
the minority in which this is not so is growing. The propor[tion]
of wives earning as much as, or more than, their husbands,
increased from 3.6 per cent to 8 per cent between 1968 an[d]
1977. Indeed, if full time women workers are compared wi[th]
their full time working husbands, the proportions have rise[n]
from 5 per cent to 14.5 per cent[2]. Even where wives' earni[ngs]
are considerably less than their husband's, they may be an
essential contribution to family finances. Indeed the earnin[gs]
of one third of wives make up 30-50 per cent of family
incomes[3].

Table 7. Economic Activity of Married Couples by Family Size*

Great Britain 1980 Economic activity of husband and wife	Percentages All with dependent children	Number of dependent children				All wit[h] depend[ent] childre[n]
		1	2	3	4 or more	
Husband working						
Wife — working: full time	15⌉ 51	19⌉ 50	13⌉ 54	11⌉ 49	9⌉ 38	41⌉ 6[0]
part time	36⌋	31⌋	40⌋	37⌋	29⌋	24⌋
— unemployed	2	2	3	2	2	[ ]
— economically inactive	39	39	38	40	44	2[ ]
Total	92	92	94	91	84	9[ ]
Husband unemployed						
Wife — working:	2	2	2	1	2	[ ]
— unemployed	Ø	Ø	Ø	Ø	NIL	[ ]
— economically inactive	3	2	2	5	9	[ ]
Total	5	5	4	6	12	[ ]
Husband economically inactive						
Wife — working	1	1	Ø	1	1	[ ]
— unemployed	Ø	Ø	NIL	Ø	NIL	[ ]
— economically active	2	2	1	2	3	[ ]
Total	2	3	2	2	4	[ ]
BASE = 100%	3632	1360	1556	525	191	223[4]

*NOTE: This table refers to married couples with husbands and wiv[es]
working age (husbands 16-64; wives 16-59): economic activity of
husbands by economic activity of wives by number of children.

Source: Previously unpublished data from the 1980 General House[hold]
Survey Corresponding to tables 5.8 and 5.9, General Household Su[rvey]
1979 (HMSO) 1981).

An increasing proportion of families are reliant on two earners — a characteristic which varies according to the age and number of children in the family. Table 7 shows that a half of one child families currently have two earners, but that this drops to 38 per cent in four child families. In contrast 66 per cent of families without children currently rely on two incomes and in the case where the wife in such couples is aged 16-29 this rises as high as 84 per cent[4].

As we have illustrated however, in the previous section, the birth of a child, or the need to care full time for dependent relatives, will mean that at certain times in the family life cycle many two earner families must rely on one earner. For example only 29 per cent of families with a pre school child have two earners, in contrast to 68 per cent where the youngest child is over ten[5]. And at the other end of the life cycle caring for elderly relatives or an elderly spouse may reduce the number of earners on which the family can rely.

Paradoxically such losses occur at a time when many families will, of necessity, be accepting additional financial responsibilities. Serious though this income loss is in relative and/or absolute terms, it is not systematically recognised in social security provisions or in the tax system. Child benefit and the married man's tax allowance for instance are available to families whether or not the wife works. And invalid care allowance is not available to married women on the grounds that 'they might be at home anyway'[6]. Yet it is clear that the loss of a second earner can have substantial financial consequences. A small scale study of families caring for handicapped elderly people recently estimated that the 'cost' of losing the wife's earnings in this situation could amount to some £4,500 per annum[7].

Even when married women are in work their contribution to family income will, as we have shown, usually be lower than a man's. This is in part a result of their discontinuous employment profiles. Additionally, however, it results from both the patterns and type of work they are able to obtain.

We have already noted the increase in part time work amongst married women, as a response to family responsibilities. But part time workers appear to be low paid in relation to other workers. The Low Pay Unit, for example, showed that in 1979, 75 per cent of part time women workers earned less than £1.50 per hour, in contrast to 47 per cent of full time women workers and only 12.5 per cent of full time male workers[8]. Similarly, an analysis of the 1977 New Earnings

Survey shows that in all industries where women are over-represented the earnings gap is greater and the level of hou earnings lower, for part time workers[9].

In addition, women's earnings are lower than men's in ger and have in fact fallen back recently, after advances in the wake of the Equal Pay Act. Today they are on average 73 per cent of men's[10]. Clearly such differences create specia difficulties for female lone parents (who are as we noted f less reliant on earnings) and may in some instances mean women unwillingly taking full time work (where it is available) in order to achieve a particular level of income[1]

Family responsibilities also lead an unknown number of women to undertake paid employment in the home. The information we have on the economic situation of homeworkers is severely limited, but it does suggest that f many women their earnings from such employment are a important addition to family finances. Thirty one per cen respondants to a survey of toy makers said that their earn played a **major** role in the family income[12] and only 18 p cent of another sample saw their income as merely supplementing their pensions or helping with the 'little extras'[13].

It would seem that many homeworkers are **very** low paid indeed, although there are some better paid 'professionals The Low Pay Unit reported 50 per cent of respondents in survey in April 1979 earning less than 40p per hour and t thirds earning less than 60p[14]. A year later a Department Employment study estimated that average hourly earning homeworkers in manufacturing work was 70p-75p, whilst for sewing and related jobs they estimated a mean rate of per hour[15].

At that time the average rate for full time women worker manufacturing industries was 183p per hour, and for tho miscellaneous service industries 147p per hour[16].

While there is a growing recognition of the cost of travel many workers, homeworking may also entail **extra expen** for the employees, for example, for heating, lighting and electricity to run machines. Few employers, however, ap to pay expenses.

The patterns and type of work which married women, ar particularly mothers, are frequently constrained to accep therefore may have severe financial disadvantages for the and for their families. We shall show in the next section how women's employment experiences also have longer term consequences.

The family responsibilities of men, although rarely considered, also appear to have an impact on patterns of work, though to a lesser extent than for women.

Fathers in large families for example tend to work longer hours than those in smaller families[17]. Similarly, a disproportionate number of shiftworkers in this country are in the 25-44 age group[18]. Financial commitments are often greatest for this group, and for most men relate directly to the presence of children. There is little doubt that much of the motivation to work overtime and shifts comes from financial pressures. The average earnings of all male shiftworkers in manual occupations are 17 per cent greater than those for day workers in similar occupations[19] and overtime represented over 14 per cent of total gross weekly earnings in 1980[20].

It is clear from the discussion so far that earnings do not necessarily mesh with family responsibilities. Fathers in large families for example have lower hourly earnings than fathers in smaller families[21]. Furthermore, and in some cases even with **two** parents in work, an increasing number of families are forced to turn to state support, in the form of family income supplement, to bring their earnings up to an acceptable level[22]. In March 1981 there were over 103,000 families drawing family income supplement (FIS) and of these, 50,000 were two parent families[23]. The availability of FIS is clearly an explicit recognition of the inadequacy of wages alone for such families.

Unemployment and income loss

Despite the provision of state benefits unemployment of the family head is still associated with loss óf income. And financial difficulties are certainly a common experience amongst the unemployed. In a recent survey of unemployed men almost 80 per cent of the respondants mentioned shortage of money as one of the worst aspects of being out of work[24]. It appears that financial difficulties may be particularly significant for larger families. One researcher concluded that the extent of financial difficulties amongst large families, despite the fact that they received higher benefits, showed:

"More clearly than before that the gearing of benefits is insufficient to meet the needs of those with large families."[25]

65

Much research has demonstrated that the experience of unemployment is not evenly distributed[26]. In particular, workers in low paid and unskilled manual occupations are particular risk of losing their jobs and of remaining unemployed for long periods[27]. Similarly, as we have seen unemployment is not necessarily an isolated incident but forms part of a pattern of employment marked by insecur and disadvantage. These relationships are compounded, as describe later, by a benefit system which effectively discriminates against those workers at greater risk of unemployment and the long term unemployed.

The concentration of unemployment amongst families is a matter of considerable concern, as the protection offered second earner is much less prevalent in these families than in the total working population. Only 39 per cent of the v of men in the DHSS cohort study said that they were economically active, compared with 58 per cent for all wi at that time. And their unemployment rate was high at 17 cent compared with 4 per cent for wives in general[28]. Suc findings confirm the conclusions of earlier research which suggested that 'the average family suffering unemploymer not cushioned by the earnings of secondary workers (or a least wives) to anything like the extent suggested by the h incidence of secondary workers in the economy as a whol The cushion is particularly thin for the families of unemp unskilled workers, especially those with three or more children'[29].

Employment, earnings and later life

We have focussed so far on the economic consequences o particular patterns of work for families with dependent children or other relatives. But equally at the other end c life cycle, the risk of poverty in old age is much reduced pensioner continues to work[30]. We have already drawn attention to the declining activity rates amongst both me women over 60 and part of the explanation for this is no doubt the extension of state and occupational pension schemes. In the future retirement pensioners will increasi be in receipt of an earnings related component to the sta pension or one or more occupational pensions, but this d not mean that the financial problems of old age have bee solved. In real terms national insurance pensions have increased from 37 to 42 per cent of net income at averag earnings for a married couple, from 1970 to 1980[31]. Ann although some substantial advances have been made by t

1975 Social Security Pensions Act it will be well into the next century before most pensioner couples have a pension which is even half of average earnings[32].

Part of the increase in early retirement and the reduction in activity rates after retirement can, however, be explained in terms of a shortage of jobs. Such involuntary 'inactivity' will exacerbate the already serious problem of poverty amongst the retired population unless pension provisions are improved. A 1977 survey of people who had retired early found, for example, that many were experiencing financial difficulties and nearly one half of the men received means tested benefits[33].

Employment and other incomes

Employment is not only a source of current earnings, it is also an important link to income related benefits. However, the availability of these is still limited and eligibility is affected by the patterns of work we have been describing.

Eligibility criteria for national insurance benefits provided by the state — which include maternity, sickness and unemployment benefits plus retirement pensions are complex and cannot be covered in detail here. Entitlement is related to a range of factors which differ for individual benefits. The majority of them are, however, dependent on contribution records, which in their turn will be affected by level of earnings, continuity of employment, hours of work, and so on[34]. Many workers are therefore not entitled to certain national insurance benefits because they have made no contributions, whilst others receive reduced benefits because their contributions are inadequate. The nature of maternity benefits clearly illustrates the interrelationship of particular patterns of employment and benefit entitlement. There are three elements to the provisions. The state system provides a maternity grant of £25 (unchanged since 1969) and a maternity allowance paid weekly for a minimum of 18 weeks (11 before and 7 after confinement). The rate of allowance is currently £22.50 per week. Employers provide maternity pay for 6 weeks at 90 per cent of gross weekly salary. This is, however, ultimately financed through the State Maternity Pay Fund. Entitlement to maternity grant, previously linked to one's own or one's husband's contributions, is now non-contributory and available to all pregnant women. It is estimated that an additional 60,000 women will be eligible because of this change.[35]

The other two provisions depend on the claimant's own w
record. Of the 302,700 women who received benefits in
1979, 48 per cent qualified for the maternity grant alone[3]
Only 48 per cent of a recent sample of over 1,000 women
had done paid work in the twelve months before the birth
their child satisfied the hours and service required for
maternity pay[37]. A woman must have been continuously
employed for at least 104 weeks immediately before the 1
week before expected confinement, and work 16 hours or
more a week. If she works between 8 and 16 hours a week
qualifies only after 5 years of continuous service. Part tim
workers who are inclined to have worked for shorter perio
and/or working women with more than one child have
therefore been found to be markedly less likely to receive
maternity pay. For the women in the sample the median
minimum six weeks pay represented around £240 — a not
unsubstantial contribution to family finances prior to the
of a child when financial pressures are clearly increasing[38]

Eligibility for unemployment benefit is similarly affected
patterns of work. Theoretically an unemployed married m
entitled to unemployment benefit for one year after whic
must then rely on means tested supplementary benefit. B
entitlement to the benefit is again dependent on recent w
history. As it has been suggested, 'the national insurance
scheme is constructed on the assumption that unemploym
is an occasional, short term, social accident for people wi
regular earnings. . .'[39]

With rising levels of unemployment an increasing proport
of unemployed people are running out of contribution
entitlement to a national insurance benefit and are becom
either partially or totally dependent on supplementary be
At the end of 1980 half of unemployed claimants were n
receiving any unemployment benefit, more than a third c
unemployed (35 per cent) were totally dependent on mea
tested benefits and just over 15 per cent were not receivir
any benefit at all[40]. In May 1980, of those not receiving
unemployment benefit 47.7 per cent had exhausted their
entitlement and 28.6 per cent had a deficiency in their
national insurance contribution record.[41]

The long term unemployed are at a particular disadvanta
since alone among groups on supplementary benefit they
cannot qualify for the long term rate — currently some £
higher than the short term rate[42]. This is despite the fact
a number of studies of unemployed claimants — especial
those with children — have shown them to be amongst th
most hard pressed groups[43].

Low pay, part time work and intermittent employment records will also have often profound implications for future pension rights. We have already commented on the risk of poverty in old age today and noted that the improvements introduced in the new pension scheme will be some time coming. But pension rights are still dependent on contribution records and level of earnings, and there are new provisions concerning entitlement to basic pension for those not currently working because of qualifying 'home responsibilities' such as the care of children. In addition, the earnings related part of the pension will be based on the 20 'best' years of earnings, and will be 'dynamised' by a complex formula[44]. And once pensions are in payment they are linked to earnings rules of various sorts.

It is evident from this that the relation of employment patterns to pensions within the state scheme is complex. This is overlain by the increasing role of occupational pensions which are an important part of all occupational benefits.

Other employment related benefits

An increasing number of employees receive occupational pensions and other benefits, often misleadingly called 'fringe benefits'. Such additions to earnings may form an important part of an employee's total 'pay'[45]. Many of these additional benefits are unevenly distributed amongst the work force and typically not available to those who arguably need them most — the low paid, part time workers and those in insecure employment. One survey, for example, found that though 71 per cent of establishments offered pension benefits greater than those in the state scheme, in only 38 per cent were part time workers eligible. For sick pay 72 per cent of firms had schemes which bettered social security provisions, but in only 61 per cent were part timers eligible[46].

Similarly, in the same way that earnings in retirement lessen the risk of poverty, so does the receipt of an occupational pension[47]. But manual workers and women are particularly disadvantaged in the receipt of occupational pensions. Indeed an analysis of the 1975 General Household Survey showed that whereas half the men in a sample received an occupational pension, this was true of only one third of spinsters, one fifth of widows and only 4 per cent of married women[48]. It is worth noting here that the pension implications of the call for increased flexibility in working life are relatively neglected in the debate.

The association of private pension schemes with particular

firms or organisations currently disproportionately affects
women. If greater job mobility is demanded of workers in
future, these effects will be more widespread and will incre
the pressure for adaptation of such schemes[49].

Other benefits, such as maternity, and much more rarely
paternity, provisions are also important aspects of the qua
of working life. Yet these too are unevenly distributed and
often poorly understood. The study of maternity rights
mentioned earlier for example, noted that though a major
of women reported that their husbands had taken time of
work around the time of the birth only 13 per cent of
these fathers had had special paid leave — most commonly
amongst the higher grade non manual workers. For father
manual occupations unpaid absence was a much more
common arrangement. The author also noted that many
women and small firms were ignorant of even the minimu
legal entitlement to maternity leave[50].

Employment, financial incentives and the younger worke

So far we have focussed on the employment patterns of m
and women and their relative contributions to family fina
In addition, many families contain children over 16, who
or may not be in employment. There is in fact little
information available on the relationship between the fam
circumstances of young people and their decision to enter
labour market or stay at school[51]. But with today's high l
of unemployment, amongst those under 18 in particular,
feel it is an area which deserves some attention.

Youth unemployment must impose additional financial
burdens on some families, whilst the lack of qualification
profound implications for an individual's employment
prospects. But the decision by a young person to enter th
labour force or to obtain further education or training, w
affected by a number of factors. The relative financial
incentives available in either case will certainly be importa

The system of financial support for young people over 16
is complex. For those staying on at school from low inco
families, some education authorities provide educational
maintenance allowances. By no means all authorities mak
such provisions, however, and rates of allowance and
qualifying conditions vary from authority to authority.
Currently the ILEA pays EMAs at a maximum of about £
per week — depending on parents' incomes[53]. For those
enter further education there are local authority discretio

awards which also vary between authorities. Where children remaining at school are in families receiving Supplementary Benefits the child allowance continues to be paid up to the age of 19. However, it should be stressed that for over 70 per cent of young people full time education finishes at 16[54].

Presently for those who leave school and cannot find employment there are two major alternatives: a place with the youth opportunities programme (YOP) or unemployment[55]. A place on YOP is accompanied by a training allowance of £25 per week, whilst unemployed school leavers are entitled to a supplementary benefit of £16.85 per week from the end of the summer holidays. At the end of December 1981 one in every two under 18 year olds seeking work were either unemployed or on the Youth Opportunities Programme[56].

The new training scheme described earlier will offer a year's training to all jobless school leavers, and is to be implemented in 1982 gradually replacing the Youth Opportunities Programme.

There are a number of controversial issues surrounding this initiative. It is argued, for example, that it is mistaken to discuss and/or plan training for young unemployed 16-18 year olds separately from a wider debate about the structure of, and particularly the resources for, tertiary training and education overall.

The weekly allowance has also proved controversial. It has now been decided that school leavers entering the trial places from September this year will receive £25 per week — the same as they presently receive on YOP. If they can be snown to have 'unjustifiably' refused a place they will forfeit supplementary benefit for six weeks. Parents will continue to receive child benefit for unemployed 16 year olds not on the scheme and any other benefits they receive will take account of their responsibility for the older child[58].

Social consequences

Paid employment is not only a source of current income — direct or indirect, generous or not it also provides a range of intrinsic rewards for a large number of people. Conversely some of the patterns of employment and unemployment that we have been describing may have unintended negative effects on individual and family well being. However, whereas the economic effects of employment and unemployment are often relatively specific, more easily quantified and indeed more often measured, the social effects relate to a range of comp issues about which specific research evidence is frequently patchy. The picture is therefore incomplete and at times controversial but the issues are nevertheless important.

Whether employment is satisfying or not and the corollary this — whether unemployment is damaging or not — is the result of a complex mix of factors internal and external to the job and closely related to family circumstances.

Employment

At the most obvious level, and despite enormous improvements since the turn of the century, industrial inju disease and death still exact a terrible toll with clear implications for families. In the first quarter of 1980 there were 76,776 accidents, resulting in 131 deaths[60]. As these only the reported and recorded figures, the true totals are likely to be higher and to these must be added the heavy to from occupational diseases. In addition to the loss suffered families where deaths occur, and the financial consequence extended sickness absence, home based nursing care will als be provided in many cases. There is also evidence that some occupational health hazards may be transmitted to other family members via for example dust in clothing.[61] But employment also has many positive, though less visible, effects.

As we have already noted, it is not a straightforward exerci to identify why people work. Obviously, the majority will take paid employment to earn current income, but it is clea not money alone that is at issue. This is suggested by the considerable number of people working for incomes lower than they would receive if they relied on state benefits. In 1979 there were 150,000 families with a head in full-time work or self-employed earning an income lower than the le of supplementary benefit.[62]

In the present cultural milieu paid employment is still the most important source of status and identity for many peo — both men and women. To be employed is to be seen to b contributing to society. For many their employment is a source of satisfaction, support and friendship, however apparently menial the job seems to observers. Clearly for some people these aspects are as, if not more, important th income, though the level of satisfaction with work and particular aspects such as income, expressed in survey resul do vary by age, sex, marital status and occupation.[63]

In general it would appear that paid employment affords protection against depression in both men and women. The work of Brown and Harris for example, has demonstrated that being at home with young children makes women especially vulnerable to depression and mental illness and that paid employment outside the home was associated with a reduced risk.[64] A number of other studies, including the EOC study of shiftworking noted earlier, have reported that working women with and without children are consistently less likely to register feelings of stress on a number of items, including anxiety, tiredness, inability to sleep etc, than non working women.[65] However, it should be noted that existing illhealth may clearly prevent/discourage a woman from working.

Similarly, as we discuss below in more detail, a number of studies have reported 'better' mental health amongst employed men than unemployed. There have, however, been few studies of the relationship between men's employment and mental health in relation to their family responsibilities. It is therefore difficult to identify whether the presence of children affects their experience of work, though some tentative comments can be made from the results of related work.

Patterns of work and well being

We have already described the ways in which family responsibilities may influence the patterns of employment of both men and women but the social implications of these patterns are complex and the subject of considerable debate and controversy.

The effects of unsocial hours are perhaps the least controversial aspect of the debate and it should be noted that some over-time and some part time work may involve 'unsocial hours'. A GMWU discussion document recently attempted to qualify how unsocial different 'shift' patterns are[66]. Table 8 gives some indication of the results.

The possibility that shiftwork may have direct effects on health and safety and on family relationships is, however, more controversial and the evidence in the different areas is relatively limited. There is some evidence, for example, that shiftwork can affect sleep patterns; lead to increased fatigue; cause or exacerbate gastric and digestive problems; and increase the risk of serious accidents[67]. There has been only one major study of the relationship between shiftwork and mortality. This study found higher standardised mortality rates amongst both present and ex shiftworkers than one would expect amongst the general population.[68] A number

Table 8. How unsociable is shift work

	Unsocial hours			
	As a % of working hours	As a % of total hours in year	No. of Sat. and Suns. worked	No. of ni shifts
Day work	nil	nil	nil	nil
Double-day shift (or alternating shift)	36.8	7.8	nil	nil
3-shift non-continuous	58.3	12.4	nil	77
3-shift continuous (or 4 crew shift)	68.3	15.4	71	74
permanent nights	100.0	21.3	nil	233

Source: GMWU Research Department

of studies have suggested that family life can suffer if one both partners work long and/or unsocial hours. In one sma scale study of bus drivers working flexible shifts 'on averag third of the bus drivers and their wives/husbands experien severe stress on their relationships'[69]. In a very different context, a similarly small scale study of hospital doctors argued that their heavy work involvement may lead to fatl feeling deprived, mothers frustrated and the child(ren) neglected[70]. Similarly it is argued that the particular probl of separation and uncertainty associated with life in the ar forces may explain the high divorce rate among married couples in the services[71].

The evidence for adverse effects may be patchy but the arguments have been accepted to the extent that a numbe preventive and compensatory mechanisms have been introduced, to reduce the possible adverse effects. These include reduced hours, special health facilities and longer holidays between shifts.

Attitudes to shiftwork/unsocial hours are perhaps predict but interesting nevertheless. In the EOC survey there was widespread **approval** of men working shifts and only a qu of men and women expressed opposition to night shifts o weekend working despite the disruption this could cause family life. There was similarly widespread **opposition** to married women working shifts, especially if they had chil — except evening shifts. This was supported by both men women, presumably because the husband was assumed to available to mind the children[72]. In this context it is interesting to note that the women doing evening shifts in the EOC survey registered the lowest levels of stress[73].

Some commentators argue that shiftwork may have many positive aspects and in particular provides an opportunity for certain kinds of leisure and increased involvement with family and community activities. For example, the NEDO survey showed that many men with young families, whose wives were not working, found that double day shifts (especially) allowed them more time with their families[74]. However, other research suggests that shiftworkers in fact participate less in organisations, attend fewer meetings and are less likely to hold public offices[75]. There is also evidence that the degree of job satisfaction felt by shiftworkers may be to some extent a function of the attitude of their families[76]. If the family's attitudes are negative, then satisfaction tends to be lower.

The social consequences of women's work

We have already discussed at some length the particular patterns of work and the constraints women experience due to family responsibilities. As we also noted the employment of married women, particularly mothers, is an area of widely diverging views. There are a number of strongly debated aspects of the possible consequences of the changing employment profiles of women, three of which will be addressed in this section.

Health status. It is suggested that as women's employment profiles move closer to men's, so their health experience will begin to mirror that of men's. Women have on average a longer life expectancy than men and mortality rates for males are higher at every age than those for females. In particular, in England and Wales, the death rate due to coronary heart disease in men between 35 and 44 nearly doubled between 1950 and 1973 in which year 41 per cent of all male deaths in the age range 35 to 44 were due to cardiovascular disease[77]. Will women's participation in the formal labour market lead to a similarly much increased risk of physical ill health and in particular stress related disease?

We have already seen that employment seems to protect women from depression and other signs of stress and the data for effects on physical health are very limited. However, what little there is, is a cause for concern, but it also points to the process which may be at work. In a large scale longitudinal study in America working married women were found to have

75

a substantially increased risk of heart disease compared to working single women and non working women, but this increased risk was closely associated with the number of children the women had[78]. It would appear that problems associated with the difficulties of combining the demands of work and family responsibilities.

A recent British study noted earlier clearly supports this explanation. In this study full time women factory workers exhibited more signs of stress than part time workers, but these women worked full time rather than part time largely for financial reasons and for this reason they often 'felt the must continue to work in the factory however much they disliked the job'[79]. Characteristically the incidence of stress related diseases amongst men has not been studied in relation to their work/family responsibilities.

Brief mention should be made of the important but little understood social consequences of homeworking since of a spheres of women's work this is certainly the area about wh we know least. For some women, homework does involve considerable risks to health, including hazards from many different chemicals, some of which are poisonous; from po ventilation when working with fibres and noxious fillings; from unguarded or heavy duty machinery for which the wi in many homes is inadequate, increasing the risk of fire and electric shock[80].

The Health and Safety at Work Act gave homeworkers the same statutory protection as other workers, but their abilit to enforce these rights is severely restricted[81]. Similarly, ho working will provide precious few of the intrinsic rewards of paid employment mentioned earlier, particularly the social contact. Although clearly 'homework' such as the sale of cosmetics and kitchenware brings contact with others. One the few studies of homeworkers recorded that few of their small and unrepresentative sample expressed much sense of personal satisfaction or fulfilment in their jobs. However, homework did allow them sought-after flexibility in relatic to domestic arrangements[82].

As noted earlier, an increasing number of jobs — at differer income levels — may be carried out within the home and it would be misleading to suggest that all homeworking is inherently dangerous or for that matter, isolating. While so types of homework are associated with disadvantages of different kinds, others may enable a more satisfactory integration between home and work, and hence lead to significant social gains.

76

Marital Relationships. The second area of concern in regard to women's employment relates to the possible effects on marriage. Once again the evidence is patchy and contradictory. For example, studies in America have reported higher levels of depression amongst men with working wives[83] but replications in this country do not support this result[84]. To the extent that wives' earnings reduce financial pressures in the family they may be expected to reduce potential conflict, but there will obviously be a range of important variables, including the degree of agreement over the working patterns of both partners; the nature of child care arrangements; the nature of the actual work undertaken and the degree of stress involved in the employment itself.

It is also pertinent to note that marital problems may as easily arise from the consequences of a particular woman's lack of paid employment and indeed may result from strains introduced by the man's employment — or lack of it. In relation to marital problems in particular it would seem that the general relationship between work and family responsibilities for all family members may be a more fruitful focus than that on women's employment per se.

Children. The third and final area of concern in relation to maternal employment, which will be briefly addressed here, relates to the effects on children — perhaps the most controversial of all areas and one in which, above all others, widely expressed opinions are more common than facts.

A number of reviews of research evidence in this field have concluded that the overall picture is so confused that, in the words of one commentator 'one can say almost anything one desires about the children of employed mothers and support the statement by some research study'[85]. The longitudinal study of children begun in 1958 does provide some data which above all places these issues in a relative context. This material suggests that although children whose mothers had worked before they started school had slightly lower reading and arithmetic scores and were 'slightly less well adjusted', than children with non working mothers, the differences were much smaller if the mother worked after the children started school and in any event these differences were insignificant. when compared with the relationship between attainment and social class[86]. Research has suggested that children of working mothers perceive sex roles in a much less stereotyped way than children whose mothers do not work[87].

The belief that young children in particular need the constant companionship of their mothers underlies many of the negative attitudes towards working mothers in general and parent families in particular. In contrast the work of Rutter and others suggests that the well being of children with working mothers, may depend more directly on the quality substitute care, the reason for the mother working, her attitudes towards work and obviously the characteristics of individual child[88]. One further area of concern which shoul be noted is the possible effects of female employment on the health of an unborn child. Though an important focus for further investigation, the evidence that is presently availabl difficult to interpret, except perhaps where it relates specifically to chemical hazards.[89]

The difficulties of combining work responsibilities may, however, be reflected in parents' own perception of their involvement with children. A recent EEC survey for examp found that a majority of parents thought that neither they nor other parents, spend enough time with children today, many would welcome the extension of more flexible kinds working arrangements to enable them to have more contac with their children[90].

In the context of maternal employment in general, a recen report from the Central Policy Review Staff concluded tha

"Research findings do not suggest that when mothers go ou work, such things as their own and their family's health, th children's level of achievement and attendance at school ar their social adjustment are impaired."[91]

Unemployment

Employment may therefore have negative and/or positive outcomes for families. The actual nature of the impact on health and well being is the result of a complex interplay o several factors. The impact of unemployment is similarly affected by a range of factors. In some cases, for instances the job that is lost could have been so stressful that unemployment is a welcome relief, particularly if it does n entail financial difficulties. In the short term at least, these reduced for some families by high redundancy payments a or the availability of savings. It may also be the case that some of the difficulties associated with male unemployme are resolved within a family by the wife finding employme which provides financial and other rewards. This may or m not of course be 'acceptable' to the husband. However, as have already described the wives of the unemployed are in less likely to work than wives in general[92].

78

Studies of the effects of unemployment have therefore recorded instances where the health and general well being of the unemployed and/or their spouses has actually improved[93]. However, such cases would appear, on the basis of existing research evidence, to be the exception rather than the rule. For most people unemployment appears to be a debilitating experience and it is not an 'individual' one. The vast majority of unemployed men and women, young and old, are living in families, and there may be more than one person experiencing unemployment. Other family members will be affected, but to different degrees. It has also been demonstrated that the nature of family relationships is one of the most powerful factors mitigating the adverse consequences of unemployment[94].

It should, however, be stressed that in the past unemployment has been seen very much as an individual experience. Much of the research, particularly in the last few decades, has been focussed on the individual who has lost the job and in particular on men. It is only very recently that the family dimension of unemployment, and/or the effects of female unemployment, have been given explicit attention[95]. Indeed a great deal of our limited insight into the possible effects on families comes from studies undertaken during the great depression[96], and considerable social and economic changes have occurred since then. The effects of these are in themselves problematic. For example, it is argued that the financial position of the unemployed is much improved today providing more support. Conversely, the much vaunted break up of extended families may mean less support is available.

Few people would deny that for the majority of people unemployment is a traumatic experience: more controversial, however, is the question of whether unemployment directly affects both health and wellbeing and if it does so, what is the magnitude of this effect[97]. Certainly the disabled and the chronically sick are at greater risk of losing their jobs or of being unemployed for long periods[98]. It should not therefore be surprising to find a greater incidence of ill health amongst the unemployed. But there is a growing body of research which suggests that unemployment is associated with an increased risk of ill health, emotional disturbance and family breakdown.

As has already been noted a number of recent studies have suggested that unemployed and/or redundant workers are more vulnerable to psychiatric disorder than those in employment. One researcher commented that their symptoms were often sufficient to have admitted the individual to hospital[99], whilst another study with unemployed school leavers concluded that they were more adversely affected adult unemployed, especially when it came to measures of hostility[100]. Though few studies have involved wives, there evidence that particularly in adverse financial circumstanc similar process of psychological deterioration could be identified[101].

Unemployment has also been associated with a deteriorati in physical health. One American study found various indications of increased ill health amongst a group of men unemployed for 26 months, compared with a control grou work. Levels of blood pressure, serum cholesterol and seru acid all increased significantly and returned to normal afte re-employment. There was also an increased frequency of peptic ulcers amongst the men *and* their wives[102]. These changes are clear indicators of increased stress and increas proneness to disease preceeding and during unemploymen However, so far they have not been replicated in other studies[103].

Research on the effects of parental unemployment on chil has been reviewed in a forthcoming paper by Madge[104]. W in the 1930s recorded the predictable effects of material deprivation on health, development and educational attainment, but recent work is much more limited. Howev it has suggested an association between unemployment an behavioural disorders in young people[105]. Similarly poor educational attainment has been identified amongst childr of the unemployed[106]. A study in the mid 1970s found th parental unemployment doubled the risk of young childre being admitted to hospital and that the poverty caused by unemployment was a contributory factor[107]. Furthermor several studies have suggested that unemployment is at lea associated with, if not in fact contributing to, child abuse

The effect of youth unemployment on family relationship similarly an area about which we know very little, but one which should perhaps be the focus of more concern. It wo seem that in some cases it can generate severe tensions within the home[109].

A further cause for concern is the possible association bet unemployment and children being taken into the care of local authority. In this area too, there is very little researc particularly on a national scale. But in two small scale surveys in Birmingham and Portsmouth a large number of parents (around 50 per cent) were unemployed at the tim

Handwritten margin notes:

Health

link in with previous statement about stressful employment

children

health + child

youth ue

80

Children *difficulty of studies*

their children were taken into care. Unemployment, it was concluded, and the poverty associated with it, had contributed to the children going into care[110].

Much of the research on the social consequences of unemployment is based on small samples, usually of the unemployed themselves. Few of them have controls and even fewer follow the individuals over time. It is therefore difficult to say what effects are caused directly by unemployment, but there are good reasons to suppose that unemployment would cause considerable strains within families and could directly affect health and well being. As we have already described, unemployment will mean a fall in living standards for many families, which will be particularly severe for those unemployed for long periods. The loss of a job may also mean the loss of status and social networks for many people which can lead to damaging stress. While some families may resolve these difficulties, for others they may impose an intolerable burden. The presence of particular circumstances such as responsibility for an elderly and/or frail relative, may for example be particularly important, and the effects of unemployment on the increasing number of families providing such care can only be guessed at.

It should also be noted that the possible adverse effects of unemployment may not be confined to those families directly experiencing it. As unemployment rises, more and more people fear redundancy and in particular the financial problems this will entail. Between June and September 1980 for instance, Gallup recorded a rise from 27 per cent to 38 per cent of people who thought their own jobs were under threat[111]. This figure has most probably increased again and such fears no doubt generate considerable anxiety within many families.

Employment trends and the family: looking to the future

We have highlighted a number of issues surrounding the ways in which family members decide, as individuals and as a family, on who works and for how long. But how are these patterns likely to change in the future?

Although we have acknowledged the way in which women's employment behaviour has changed over time, we have still in some senses presented a static picture. A more comprehensive view would involve considering the way in which women's, and men's, employment profiles are changing in relation to events in the family life cycle. To what extent will

81

tomorrow's women give up paid employment when their children are born, and for how long? How will these interruptions to employment affect levels of earnings ove person's lifetime, and their career opportunities? Similarl we have already stressed, it is impossible to be precise abc the implications of future employment trends for the economic and social well being of families. However, a number of critical issues can be identified.

It is predictable that the future will involve considerable changes in both the nature and availability of employmer and in family life though the precise forms of the change: more difficult to predict. We discuss the question of wher responsibilities should lie in relation to adaptation to the changes in the conclusion, but here note that in both sph of life — work and home — considerable adaptations will necessary.

A family's ability to adapt is related to many factors, but economic well being, as we have seen with unemploymer may be critical. In the future higher levels of unemploym and the impact of technological change may demand grea adaptability.

As we have already noted the need for job mobility may increase considerably in the next decade — a trend with important social and economic implications. Already, as have described, the unequal geographical distribution of employment opportunities is marked. Successive attempt government to regenerate older industrial areas and inner have had little success and there are growing calls for peo to 'move' to work. The Manpower Services Commission example has recently increased the transfer grant availabl those without work or facing redundancy to encourage mobility. The present level of £1,350 for a married coup with one or more children plus the removal expenses anc contribution towards the legal expenses of selling and bu a house, will go some way to compensate for the cost of moving. However, there are other problems in relation, f example, to education, and perhaps in particular the pro of support for elderly relatives.

Finally we should raise the question of the future availab of work for women in relation to men. Though, as we ha seen, part time work and home-work is presently poorly and often associated with other disadvantages, this need inevitably be the case. The increased availability of more flexible working time — associated with at least the disappearance of differentials between part time and full time workers, and women and men — would facilitate a more equal division of work and family responsibilities, without the considerable social and economic penalties presently involved.

Part 4

Conclusion

We have demonstrated that the relationship between employment and the family is two way. Trends in both t level, and pattern, of employment and unemployment ha affected the social and economic circumstances of famili and we have indicated how they may do so in the future. Conversely, family responsibilities affect the employmen patterns of men and women and such responsibilities can do, change over the life cycle. The complex interaction o these factors, together with changing social attitudes, hav given the lie to any idea of the typical worker as a marrie man with a non working wife and two children. Indeed, i 1979 such a 'typical' worker represented a mere 5 per ce the total labour force[1]. But what are the implications of analysis?

The paper has highlighted the fact that in these, as in oth areas, there are many contentious issues and questions of value, which facts alone are not capable of resolving. A particular case in point is the way in which families divid their employment and child care responsibilities. We hav documented the rise of two earner families and have also shown how the pattern of women's employment has bee changing, both in relation to child care and to their othe family responsibilities. Such changes are the subject of m debate and concern. For example over 15 years ago Hun survey found that whilst a majority of women would enc the right of a married woman to work, they were far less likely to do so were she responsible for children, and onl minority of women would have endorsed the right of a woman with a pre school child to work outside the hom Smaller surveys in recent years have confirmed that this issue on which views are deeply divided[3]. Perhaps becaus this, few young children have mothers who work full tim only some 5 per cent of children under 5 in 1978[4]. On th other hand an additional 20 per cent of pre school childr have mothers who work part time and the issue of adequ substitute care for all children while their mothers are at will remain a central part of any policy focussing on employment and the family.

We have demonstrated that the effects of family responsibilities are not confined to the employment of mothers. Men's employment is also affected — though in a different way. Whilst women may be held out of the labour market by their family responsibilities, so men may be drawn into it, restricting the time which they are able to spend in the family. At least part of the involvement in overtime and shiftwork evident amongst men who are more likely to have these responsibilities, arises, as we argued, from the mismatch between earnings and family responsibilities. An increasing concern with 'parental' employment would provide a welcome counterweight to the narrow focus on mothers' employment.

We have also shown that children are only one dimension of family responsibility. A growing area of concern is the position of those with elderly or handicapped dependants. Whilst there has been far less attention paid to the employment consequences of caring for such dependants, there are a number of interesting parallels with the situation of those caring for children. Caring for such dependants can affect whether or not an individual works, the hours or proximity of the job that can be taken, or the level of responsibility that can be accepted — especially if it involves geographical mobility. Paradoxically, however, whilst employment opportunities are often constrained, the need for additional income may be increased. As an Equal Opportunities Commission survey noted, 'nearly all carers have to bear extra costs for which no financial assistance is available'. These included extra transport costs, additional food and fuel costs[5]. The shifting age structure of the elderly population means that an increasing number of families will face this issue in the 1980s and 1990s. How far are those with such responsibilities enabled to work when they wish to do so by the provision of an adequate infrastructure of services in the community? How far are workers with these responsibilities helped to meet the demands of home and work by sympathetic and flexible employment policies?

The growing awareness of the implications of marriage breakdown and the increasing number of parents and children who will experience a period in a one parent family is another important theme in this paper. Such parents, mainly women, face particularly acute employment problems. For all parents, employment is both a source of income and a source of contact and status. For lone parents, as the Finer Report noted over seven years ago, employment, perhaps on a part time basis, may be as valuable for its social dimensions as for the additional income that it generates.

Equally, in relation to the position of divorcees, if the ide
self sufficiency is given greater weight as an objective in t
legislation governing financial provisions after divorce, th
will probably be changes in the way in which women viev
their own employment situation in relation to marriage.

In all these cases there are implications for employment
practices. We have, for example, highlighted the role whic
part time work currently plays in allowing workers — alth
currently mainly women — to mesh home and work
responsibilities. But we have noted many of the disadvan
that such work entails. In the future 'better quality' part
work could well prove valuable in allowing individuals to
achieve a better balance between work and home. More
generally, there is perhaps scope for extending other type
flexibility to a greater number and variety of workers. Su
changes would, however, be only an extension of existing
practices and there is a sense in which simply projecting
forward current 'solutions', may be inadequate in the ligh
the uncertainties surrounding future employment prospe
Change, if nothing else, is a predictable outcome of curre
developments.

The changes we have documented in family patterns are
place within the context of rapid shifts in the level and
patterns of employment. In some ways debates about the
future of work, and of the quality and nature of employr
have been 'technological' or individualistic in orientation
debates have, as yet, failed to include a family dimension
as we have shown, these changes have consequences not
for individuals, but also for their families. While we have
emphasised that individuals and their families adopt varic
strategies for meeting the demands of work and family, s
accommodation as can be made takes place within the
framework of public policy and trade unions' and emplo
practices.

It is not the purpose of this paper to define a role for pu
and private policy in the sphere of employment. Rather,
concern has been to show that the timely and urgent deb
on employment issues needs to be informed by a family
perspective. In practice this means a deeper understandir
the ways in which changing family patterns, roles and
obligations, have an impact on the individual's availabilit
willingness to work, and a complementary monitoring of
impact of changes in employment on individuals and the
families. Without doubt, such monitoring and evaluation

require an extension of the already substantial framework of information which focusses on the relationship between the family and work.

It has recently been argued that the three spheres of concern of this paper — the state, the family and the economy — are in a state of flux and that there is a need for a renegotiation of their respective rights and roles[6]. There is a sense in which this process is already occurring and we would suggest that the development of a family perspective is one valuable way to promote this renegotiation in the sphere of employment.

The background to the paper

We are not the first to discuss the relationship between wo
and the family and throughout the text we have reference
other work in the field. However, there is a large body of
literature to which we have not specifically made referenc
and we feel it would be proper and useful to describe the
growing foundation upon which this report has been based

The relationship between work and the family in history h
been addressed by writers such as Laslett, Shorter and
Anderson, and in more recent times, in 'community studie
such as that undertaken by Young and Wilmott.
Characteristically, such studies looked at relationships wit
the family. However, much of the earlier work focussed
specifically on maternal employment and in particular on
affects on family life and children (eg Rutter). The review
research in this field by for example Hoffman in America,
Pilling and Kellmer Pringle in the United Kingdom, are usef
sources. As with many other issues, the range of publicati
from the cohort studies provides valuable information. Th
include the publications by Butler et al, Davie et al and
Douglas et al described below.

In psychological literature, the persistent differences in me
health between men and women and married and non mar
individuals has received considerable attention. The work
Cochrane and Stopes-Roe, and Brown and Harris relate th
work to the debate about the relationship between work a
family life. A body of literature is building up looking int
the role of the housewife (Oakley), and at women with
dependants (Hunt). As concern for equal opportunities gr
material in this field accumulated; the works of Land and
are particularly valuable and the EOC itself publishes a gr
deal of valuable information. They are presently producin
series of documents on flexibility in working life.

Attention has increasingly shifted towards a work-**family**
and away from maternal employment per se. In this area
work of Kamerman and Kahn, and Moss and Fonda provi
invaluable discussions of the issues and policy options. Wh
the work of the Rapoports, the Pahls and Fogarty provide

more detailed analysis of the relationships between family functioning and parental employment. The implications of changing family structures for different policy areas, including employment, have also been addressed by researchers (George and Wilding, and Wynn) and the Committee on One Parent Families (Finer).

In parallel with the sociological interest described above there have been a number of econometric studies of the determinants of labour supply in relation to family composition, most notably the work of Greenhalgh, Joshi and others.

1
M Anderson,
Family Structure in Nineteenth Century Lancashire,
Cambridge University Press, New York, 1971

2
G B Brown and T Harris,
Social Origins of Depression: A Study of Psychiatric Disorders in Women,
Tavistock, London 1978

3
N Butler, A Osborn, S Dowling and B Howlett (forthcoming),
Britain's Five Year Olds,
Routledge, London

4
R Davie, N Butler and H Goldstein,
From Birth to Seven: Second Report of the National Child Development Study,
(1958 cohort), Longman, for National Children's Bureau, London 1972

5
J W Douglas, and J M Blomfield,
Children Under Five,
Allen and Unwin, London 1958

6
Equal Opportunities Commission,
Job Sharing: Improving the Quality and Availability of Part Time Work. Alternative Work Arrangements, number 1,
1982

7
R M Finer,
Report of the Committee on One Parent Families,
vols 1 and 2, HMSO, 1974

8
M Fogarty, R Rapoport and R N Rapoport,
Women and Top Jobs: An Interim Report,
PEP, London 1976

9
M Fogarty, R Rapoport and R Rapoport,
Sex, Career and the Family,
Allen and Unwin, London 197

10
V George and P Wilding,
Motherless Families,
Routledge, London 1972

11
C Greenhalgh,
'A Labour Supply Function fc Married Women in Great Brita
Economica
44, p 249-65, 1977

12
C Greenhalgh,
'Participation and Hours of W for Married Women in Great Britain',
Oxford Economic Papers,
vol 32, no 2, Clarendon Press,

13
L Hoffman and F Nye,
Working Mothers,
2nd edition, Jossey-Bass, New York 1978

14
A Hunt,
A Survey of Women's Employment,
HMSO, London 1968

15
A Hunt,
The Home Help Service in England and Wales,
Government Social Survey, HMSO 1970

16
H Joshi,
Secondary Workers in the Cyc Married Women and Older Workers in Employment Fluctuations, Great Britain, 1961-74:
Government Economic Servic Working Paper, no 8,
DHSS, Economic Advisers' Of London 1978

17
H Joshi and S Owen,
Demographic Predictors of Women's Work Participation in Post War Britain,
Centre for Population Studies Paper, no 81.3, University of London 1981

18
S Kamerman and A Kahn
Family Policy: Government and Families in Fourteen Countries,
Columbia University Press, New York 1978

19
S Kamerman and A Kahn,
Child Care, Family Benefits and Working Parents,
Columbia University Press, New York 1980

20
H Land,
Parity Begins At Home: Women's and men's work in the home and its effects on their paid employment,
SSRC/EOC, 1981

21
P Laslett,
The World We Have Lost,
Methuen, London 1971

22
P Moss and N Fonda, (eds),
Work and the Family,
Temple Smith, London 1980

23
A Oakley,
The Sociology of Housework,
Martin Robertson, London 1974

24
J M and R E Pahl,
Managers and their Wives: A Study of Career and Family Relationships in the Middle Class,
Allen Lane, 1971

25
D Pilling and M Kellmer-Pringle,
Controversial Issues in Child Development, Paul Elek, London 1978

26
R N Rapoport and R Rapoport,
Dual Career Families Re-examined,
Martin Robertson, London 1978

27
R N Rapoport and R Rapoport,
Working Couples,
Routledge, London 1978

28
M Rutter,
Maternal Deprivation Reassessed,
Penguin Books, Harmondsworth 1972

29
E Shorter,
The Making of the Modern Family,
Collins, 1976

30
M Wynn,
Fatherless Families,
Michael Joseph, London 1964

31
M Young and P Willmott,
The Symmetrical Family,
Routledge, London 1973

The legislative context

The relationships between work and the family which we h
discussed have developed within a complex legislative
framework that has itself been subject to considerable
amendment and will continue to be so in the future. We list
below the major Acts of Parliament which go to make up th
framework and briefly describe their most significant
provisions. There is of course a range of other legislation, su
as that concerning child care provision and taxation, which
affects these relationships to varying degrees, but which we
not describe here.

Redundancy Payments Act 1965

This Act requires an employer to make a lump sum
compensation, called a redundancy payment, to any employ
(over 18 but under 65 for a man and under 60 for a woman
who is made redundant after at least 104 weeks of reckonal
service.

Equal Pay 1970 (provisions came into force in 1975)

The Act is to eliminate discrimination between men and
women in regard to pay and other terms of employment
contracts (ie overtime, bonus and piece work, holiday and
sick pay entitlement). An individual woman has a right to
equal treatment with a man when she is employed on like
work or in a job which, even if different, has been given eq
status under job evaluation.

Contracts of Employment Act 1972

This Act gives most workers the right to a minimum period
of notice of termination of employment according to lengt
service. It also introduced the right to receive from employ
a written statement of the main terms and conditions of
employment.

Health and Safety at Work 1974

The legislation extended health and safety regulations to ev
everyone except domestic staff. A Health and Safety
Commission has been established to issue codes of conduct
consolidate existing regulations and to carry out enquiries i
major accidents. Employers have to provide workers with

safety instruction, training and supervision. It is an offence not to do so, and managers and directors can be fined.

Trade Union and Labour Relations Act 1974

This Act repealed the Industrial Relations Act 1971, and abolished its institutions, (including the Industrial Relations Court) and emergency procedures, such as union ballots. It re-enacted the unfair dismissal provisions, restored the status of unions and employers' organisations. Traditional legal immunities for certain acts undertaken in contemplation and furtherance of a trade dispute were also restored. The right not to belong to a union and the voiding of pre-entry closed shops was repealed. This Act is subject to considerable amendments under the Employment Bill mentioned earlier.

Sex Discrimination Act 1975

This Act makes it unlawful to discriminate on grounds of sex, in employment, training and education as well as in the provision of goods and services. Individuals have the right to complain to the courts and to industrial tribunals. The Equal Opportunities Commission was established to help enforce the legislation and promote sexual equality. The law covers both recruitment and existing employees in matters like promotions. Exceptions include small firms with fewer than five employees and staff in private households. It is also unlawful for a union to discriminate over the terms on which it accepts a person for membership.

Employment Protection Act 1975 (Amended 1978 — 1980)

This gives unions rights on recognition and disclosure of information from employers for collective bargaining. Employees losing wages because of short time or lay offs are entitled to certain basic payments. Workers can now officially take time off for union and public duties. People dismissed unfairly can apply to a tribunal for reinstatement or compensation. Employers must notify unions about proposed redundancies. Pregnant women are entitled to paid leave and have the right to return to work. All of these rights are subject to qualifying conditions of various sorts and some changes, particularly in rights to return to work were included in the Employment Act, 1980. The Act also set up ACAS (Advisory, Conciliation and Arbitration Service).

Race Relations Act 1976

According to the provisions of this Act, discrimination is unlawful in employment, training and related matters. Individuals have access to civil courts and industrial tribunals. A Commission for Racial Equality was set up to help individuals who believe they have been discriminated against.

An employer must also not discriminate in offering a job o
inferior terms of pay or holiday entitlement.

Wages Council Act 1979

This Act consolidates the position of Wages Councils. Thes
are independent bodies which set legal minimum rates of p
and certain other conditions for workers in selected indust
mainly catering, retailing, clothing, textiles, hairdressing an
launderies. Minimum rates are enforceable by law and
Department of Employment Wages Inspectors 'police' the
system.

References

Abbreviations

ASTMS
Association of Scientific,
Technical and Managerial Staffs

CPAG
Child Poverty Action Group

CPRS
Central Policy Review Staff

CSO
Central Statistical Office

DE
Department of Employment

DHSS
Department of Health and Social
Security

EEC
European Economic Community

EOC
Equal Opportunities Commission

FES
Family Expenditure Survey

GHS
General Household Survey

GMWU
General and Municipal Workers
Union

HMSO
Her Majesty's Stationery Office

ILEA
Inner London Education
Authority

LFS
Labour Force Survey

MRC
Medical Research Council

MSC
Manpower Services Commission

NEDO
National Economic Development
Office

OECD
Organisation for Economic
Cooperation and Development

OPCS
Office of Population Censuses and
Surveys

PSI
Policy Studies Institute

RCIDW
Royal Commission on the
Distribution of Income and
Wealth

SBC
Supplementary Benefits
Commission

SSAFA
Soldiers', Sailors' and Airmen's
Families Association

SSRC
Social Science Research Council

TGWU
Transport and General Workers'
Union

Note: All places of publication
are London except where
otherwise stated

Introduction

1
See Appendix I for a review of
the literature
2
See Appendix II for a review of
recent employment related
legislation
3
See, for example, Treasury and
Civil Service Committee
**Efficiency and Effectiveness in
the Civil Service,**
HMSO, 1982

1 Recent Trends

1
RCDIW,
Report No. 8 Fifth report on the
Standing Reference,
Cmnd. 7679, HMSO, 1979, Table
2.1
2
DE,
Background Paper No. 1 to Cmnd.
8093 'The Taxation of Husband
and Wife', Inland Revenue,
HMSO, 1980a
3
RCDIW,
Op cit, 1979, Table 2.2
4
ibid, Table 2.4
5
DE
'Labour Force Outlook to 1986',
Employment Gazette,
April, HMSO, 1981, p.167-173
6
OPCS
Labour Force Survey 1973, 1975
and 1977,
HMSO, 1980b, Table 5.4
7
A Barber,
'Ethnic Origin and the Labour
Force',
Employment Gazette,
August, 1980, Table 3
8
OPCS,
General Household Survey 1979,
HMSO, 1981a, Table 5.10
9
D Manley and P Sawbridge,
'Women at Work'
Lloyds Bank Review,
No 135, 1980
10
RCDIW, op cit, (1921-1951),
1979, Table 2.7
D Manley and P Sawbridge, op cit
(1959-1978), 1980
Employment Gazette,
February 1982 (1978-1981)
Figures are for Great Britain
seasonally adjusted at June
11
D Manley and P Sawbridge,
op cit, 1980
12
MSC,
Annual Review 1980,
1981

13
DE,
Employment Gazette,
October, 1980, Table S6
14
DE,
Employment Gazette,
1981, October, S6
15
RCDIW, op cit, 1979, para. 2
16
OPCS, op cit, 1981a, Table 5
17
RCDIW, op cit, 1979, Table
Approximately 4% of the
population were involved in
agriculture, fishing, mining an
quarrying in 1975
18
J Sleigh, B Boatwright, P Irw
and R Stanyon
The Manpower Implications
Micro-Electronic Technology
HMSO, 1979, p.5
19
RCDIW, op cit, 1979 p.33 et
20
ibid table 2.7
21
ibid p. 27, para. 2.32. For a
analysis, see G Wilkinson and
Jackson,
Public Sector Employment i
UK,
University of Leicester, 1981
22
DE,
Employment Gazette,
May, 1981, S6
23
DE,
Employment Gazette,
October, 1981, S6
24
RCDIW, op cit, 1979, Table
OPCS, op cit, 1981a, Table 5
25
DE,
'Numbers of Self-Employed
People',
Employment Gazette,
January, 1982, p 15
26
Outer Circle Policy Unit,
Policing the Hidden Econom
Outer Circle Policy Unit, 19

27
N Bosanquet and P B Doeringer,
'Is there a dual labour market in
Great Britain?.
Economic Journal,
June 1973
C Hakim,
Occupational Segregation,
Research Paper No.9 Department
of Employment, 1979
I Breughel,
'Women as a reserve army of
labour',
Feminist Review,
No. 3, 1979
28
S Shimmin, J McNally and S Liff
'Pressures on women engaged in
factory work',
Employment Gazette,
August, 1981, pp. 344-349
29
OPCS, op cit, 1981a, Table 5.10
30
ibid Table 5.11
31
ibid Table 5.4
32
ibid Tables 5.10 and 5.11
33
D Manley and P Sawbridge,
op cit, 1980, p.31
34
C Moir,
'Reply to Manley and Sawbridge',
Lloyds Bank Review, April, 1980
35
A Trown and G Needham,
'Reduction in Part-time Teaching:
implications for schools and
women teachers', EOC/University
of Lancaster, 1980, p.1
36
GMWU,
Shiftwork; a discussion document
1980
37
F Fishwick,
The Introduction and Extension
of Shiftworking, NEDO, 1980
38
C Hakim,
'Homeworking: some new
evidence',
Employment Gazette,
October, 1980
and
A Cragg and T Dawson,
Qualitative Research among

Homeworkers,
Research Paper No.21,
Department of Employment,
1981
39
P Townsend,
Poverty in the United Kingdom,
Allen Lane, 1979, pp.463-5
40
Select Committee on
Employment,
Homeworking,
First report from the
Employment Committee, Session
1981-82, HC 39, HMSO, 1981
41
A Smith,.
'The Informal Economy',
Lloyds Bank Review,
July, 1981
42
OPCS,
General Household Survey 1978,
HMSO, 1980a, Table 5.14
43
DE,
Employment Gazette,
June, 1981, Table 5.16, July
figures.
44
CSO,
Social Trends 12,
HMSO, 1981, Table 4.11
45
ibid Table 4.12
46
OPCS, op cit, 1980b, Table 5.15
Table 5.15
47
M White,
Shorter Working Time,
PSI, 1980
48
DE,
'Patterns of Holiday
Entitlement',
Employment Gazette,
December, 1981
49
M White, op cit, 1980, p.83
50
S Glynn and J Oxborrow,
Interwar Britain: a social and
economic history,
G Allen & Unwin, 1976, Table
5.4
51
ibid, p.153

52
DE,
Employment Gazette,
March, 1982, Table S22, (UK figures).
53
DE,
Employment Gazette,
January, 1982, Table 2.3 (October 1981 figures)
54
ibid, Table 2.4
55
D Eversley and A Evans (eds)
Inner City: employment and industry,
Heinemann, 1980, p.456
56
OPCS, .
Census 1981 Preliminary Report England and Wales,
HMSO, 1981b, Table C
57
OPCS,
County Monitor. Merseyside Supplement,
Ref. CEN 81 CM28/S, HMSO, 1981c, Table E
58
D J Smith,
Unemployment and Racial Minorities,
PSI, 1981, p.3
59
ibid, p.5
60
CSO, op cit, 1981, p.72 (UK figures)
61
DE,
Employment Gazette,
February, 1982, Table 2.6
Figures refer to males in GB
62
See Table 4
63
OPCS,
Monitor GHS 81/1,
1981d, Table 13. Unemployment registration procedures are to change in late 1982.
64
'TUC reckons jobless total at over 4 million',
Guardian,
13 October 1981
65
H Joshi,
'Secondary Workers in the Employment Cycle',

Economica,
1981, vol. 48, no. 149
66
OPCS, op cit, 1981a, chapter
67
SBC,
Annual Report 1979,
Cmnd 8033, HMSO, 1980, p.
68
CSO, op cit, 1981, Tables 4.2 and 4.26
69
W W Daniel,
The Unemployed Flow,
Stage I Interim Report PSI, 1
p II.33
70
ibid
71
MSC,
A Study of the Long Term Unemployed,
MSC, 1980, para. 4.1
72
Unemployment in the GHS is equivalent to registered unemployment. And see Soci Security Advisory Committee
First Annual Report
HMSO, 1982.
73
C Smee and J Stern,
The Unemployed in a period high Unemployment: Characteristics and benefit st
Government Economic Servic Working Paper No. 11, HMSC 1978, p.10
74
ibid
75
House of Commons Hansard,
Written Answers
March 1982 Vol. 19 Col. 48
76
L Rimmer,
Unemployment and the Fam
1981
and J Popay,
A Discussion of the Health ar other Social Consequences of Unemployment,
1981
Papers prepared for a seminar the WASTE (Work and Societ in the Eighties) group
Unpublished

II Future Trends

1
MSC
Manpower Review 1980, nd.
2
DE, 'Labour Force Outlook to
1986', op cit, 1981
3
Activity rates amongst this age
group will be affected by changes
in social security administration,
for example, allowing workers
over 60 to obtain long term
benefit rates, provided they do
not register as unemployed.
4
OPCS
Monitors
GHS 80/1, GHS 81/1 and LFS
82/1.
5
DE, 'Labour Force Outlook to
1986', op cit, 1981, p.168.
6
It should be noted that the most
recent General Household Survey
(1979) does not show a declining
activity rate amongst married
women with dependent children.
7
DE, 'Labour force Outlook to
1986', op cit, 1981, p.168
8
DE, 'Regional Labour Force
Outlook to 1986',
Employment Gazette,
November, 1981, p.472-476
9
R Noyce,
'Microelectronics' in
Scientific American,
September 1977
10
Department of Industry,
**Information Technology, The Age
of Electronic Information,**
1981, p.3
11
Department of Industry,
**Microelectronics: The New
Technology,**
1978
12
Cited in J Evans,
**The Implications of Micro-
electronics on Employment in
Western Europe in the 1980s,**
European Trade Union Institute,
1980, p.86

13
National Cash Register (NCR)
Annual Report 1975
14
Association of Scientific,
Technical and Managerial Staff,
**Technological Change and
Collective Bargaining, A
Discussion Document,** nd
p.20
15
J Ardill, The Guardian, 6 April
1978, quoted in C Hines and G
Searle,
Automatic Unemployment,
Earth Resources Research, 1979,
p.23
16
C Jenkins and B Sherman,
The Collapse of Work,
Eyre Methuen Ltd, 1979
17
J Sleigh, et al, op cit, and
Advisory Council for Applied
Research and Development
(ACARD),
**Technological Change: Threats
and Opportunities for the
United Kingdom,**
Cabinet Office, HMSO, 1979
18
Quoted in U Huws,
**The Impact of New Technology
on the Working Lives of Women
in West Yorkshire, Interim
Report,**
TUCRIC, Leeds, 1980
19
J Rada,
The Impact of Microelectronics,
ILO, and U Huws, ibid, 1980.
20
Quoted in Sleigh et al, op cit,
1979, p.96
21
A Walker,
'The Social Consequences of
Increasing Early Retirement',
The Political Quarterly,
January, 1982, p.61-72
22
M White, op cit, 1980
23
Unpublished MSC figures quoted
in
Unemployment Unit Bulletin,
No.1, August 1981. The forecasts
for 1983 range from 54% in the
first quarter to 68% in the second.

24
P Makeham,
'Youth Unemployment, An
examination of evidence on youth
unemployment using national
statistics',
Department of Employment
Research Paper Number 10, 1980
25
Youthaid,
Quality or Collapse,
January 1981
26
MSC,
Review of the third year of
special programmes,
1981
27
Youthaid,
Bulletin,
December 1981, No.I, p.2
28
Department of Employment,
A New Training Initiative: A
Programme for Action,
HMSO, December, 1981
29
C Hakim,
'Job Segregation: Trends in the
1970s' in
Employment Gazette,
December, 1981, p.521-529
30
ibid
31
J Marstrand,
Association of Scientific,
Technical and Managerial Staff,
quoted in C Hines and G Searle,
op cit, 1979, p.23
32
U Huws, op cit, 1980, p.44
33
ibid, p.46
34
CPRS,
Social and Employment
Implications of Microelectronics,
HMSO, 1978, p.6-7
35
See E Bird,
Information Technology: The
mpact on Women's Jobs,
EOC, 1980 for a discussion of
these issues.
36
ibid, p.67
37
ibid, p.68, for more information
contact group 'Emploi a Distance'

Post 454, Institut Auguste Co
21 Rue Descartes, 75005, Pari
38
Urwick Nexos,
The structure and Design of
Tomorrow's Office,
1980
39
E Bird, op cit, 1980
40
U Huws, op cit, 1980, p.66 an
67
41
ASTMS (nd), op cit, p.20

III EMPLOYMENT TRENDS
AND THE FAMILY: SECTIO
A: LABOUR SUPPLY AND
FAMILY RESPONSIBILITIE

1
Such cross sectional data
represent the aggregate experie
of a group of people rather tha
the actual experience of an
individual. The issue is the ext
to which individual profiles di
from the representation given
here
2
H Joshi and S Owen,
Demographic Predictors of
Women's Work Participation i
Post War Britain,
Centre for Population Studies,
1981 and DE, op cit, 1980.
3
OPCS, op cit, 1981a, Table 5.
4
ibid, Table 5.4
5
A Hunt,
A Survey of Women's
Employment, 1968
Government Social Survey,
HMSO, quoted in H Land,
Parity Begins At Home,
EOC, 1981, p.6
6
ibid
7
A survey on 'Women and
Employment' is being underta
by the Department of
Employment which replicates
Hunt's study, and, for the firs
time, includes data on
employment histories.

8
M Bone,
Pre School children and the Need for Day Care,
OPCS/HMSO, 1977, p.59

9
W W Daniel,
Maternity Rights: The Experience of Women,
PSI, 1980, Table III.II, and Table XI.I

10
S Shimmin et al, op cit, 1981

11
P Moss,
'Parents At Work' in P Moss and N Fonda (eds),
Work and the Family,
Temple Smith, quoted in H Land, op cit, 1980

12
ibid, p.28

13
OPCS,
GHS 1979,
op cit, p.76, 1981a. The exception is men with four or more dependent children.

14
R Layard, D Piachaud and M Stewart.
The Causes of Poverty,
Background Paper no.5 to the Royal Commission on the Distribution of Income and Wealth (RCDIW) report no.6,
Lower Incomes,
HMSO, 1978, Table 7.10

15
P Moss, op cit, quoting National Board for Prices and Incomes, 1970,
Hours of Work, Overtime and Shiftwork,
report no 161, HMSO, 1980
and M Young and P Willmott,
The Symmetrical Family
Routledge & Kegan Paul, 1973, p.37

16
Work on this is being undertaken by H Joshi, and at the Centre for Labour Economics

17
J Hurstfield,
Part Time Pittance,
Low Pay Review I Low Pay Unit, 1980

18
C Greenhalgh and M Stewart (forthcoming)

19
DHSS,
Growing Older,
Cmnd 8173, HMSO, 1981

20
C Rossiter and M Wicks,
Crisis or Challenge: Family Care, Elderly People and Social Policy,
Study Commission on the Family, 1982

21
EOC,
The Experience of Caring for Elderly and Handicapped Dependants: survey report,
EOC, 1980

22
A Hunt, op cit, 1968, p.109

23
A Hunt,
The Home Help Service in England and Wales,
HMSO, 1970, p.424

24
A Briggs,
Who Cares?,
unpublished, 1981

25
A Hunt, op cit, 1968, p.112

26
A Hunt,
The Elderly at Home,
OPCS/HMSO, 1978, p.63

27
L Rimmer,
'Focus on the Family',
Employment Gazette,
September, 1981

28
L Rimmer,
Families in Focus,
Study Commission on the Family, 1981
and J Haskey,
'The Proportion of Marriages Ending in Divorce',
Population Trends 27,
HMSO, 1982

29
See figure 3: Incidence of Unemployment by Marital Status

30
House of Commons Hansard, 23 July 1981, cols. 221 et seq.

31
DE, op cit, 1980, Table 9

32
House of Commons, Hansard, 23 July 1981, op cit

33
J Popay, L Rimmer and C Rossiter, (forthcoming),
A report on the circumstances of one parent families,
Study Commission on the Family, 1982

34
R Layard et al, op cit, 1978, fig 3.2

35
J Nixon,
Fatherless Families on FIS,
DHSS, HMSO, 1979, p.89

36
V George and P Wilding,
Motherless Families,
Routledge and Kegan Paul, 1972 quoted in H Land, op cit, 1981.

37
H Joshi and S Owen, op cit, 1981

38
ibid, p.13

39
W W Daniel, op cit, 1980, p.74

40
K Dunnell,
Family Formation 1976,
OPCS, HMSO, 1979, p.30, Table 6.4

41
OPCS, op cit, 1981a, Table 5.3

42
ibid table 5.3, and H Joshi and S Owen, op cit, 1981, p.13

43
C Greenhalgh,
'A Labour Supply Function for Married Women in Great Britain,
Economica,
No. 44, 1977, pp.249-265

44
A Hunt, op cit, 1968, p.77

45
W W Daniel, op cit, 1980, p.76

46
R Layard et al, op cit, 1978, p.64

47
EOC,
Third Annual Report 1978,
EOC, 1979, Table 4.2, Figures are for gross hourly earnings.

48
F Field,
Fair Shares for Families,
Study Commission on the Family, 1980, p.13

49
D Piachaud, (forthcoming)
Family Incomes since the War,

Study Commission on the F
1982

50
R Layard et al, op cit, 1978

51
M McNay and C Pond,
Low Pay and Family Povert
Study Commission on the F
1980, p.13

52
CPRS,
People and their Families,
HMSO, 1980, para 6.1.4

53
A Hunt, op cit, quoted in H
1981, op cit, 1968, p.14

54
ibid, p.78

55
K Dunnell, op cit, 1979, Tal

56
EOC, op cit, 1981

57
Law Commission,
The Financial Consequence
Divorce,
Paper No. 12, HMSO, 1981

58
W W Daniel, op cit, 1981

59
C Smee and J Stern, op cit,
1978, p.14

60
S Moylan and B Davies,
'The Disadvantages of the
Unemployed'
Employment Gazette,
August, 1980, p.832

61
A Marsh,
Women and Shiftwork
OPCS/EOC survey, HMSO,

62
ibid, p.79

63
A Hunt, op cit, 1968, quote
A Marsh, op cit, 1979, p.81

64
A Marsh, op cit, 1979

**III.B. ECONOMIC & SOCIA
CONSEQUENCES FOR
FAMILIES**

1
House of Commons Hansar
Written Answers,
27 July, 1979, col. 672

2
P Elias,
**The Joint Distribution of
Economic Activity and Earnings
of Married Couples in the UK
1968 and 1977**
Paper prepared for EOC, 1980
3
L Hamill,
**Wives as Sole and Joint
Breadwinners,**
Government Economic Service
Working Paper No.15, 1979, p.13
4
Unpublished data from 1980
GHS. Equivalent to table 5.9,
GHS 1979
5
ibid
6
HC 276,
**Social Security Provision for
Chronically Sick and Disabled
People,**
HMSO, 1974, p.20
7
M Nissel and L Bonnerjea,
**Family Care of the Handicapped
Elderly: Who Pays?**
PSI, 1982, p.56
8
J Hurstfield,
'Part Time Pittance'
Low Pay Review I,
1980, Table 3
9
New Earnings Survey, 1977,
quoted in C Leicester,
**Part-time Employment in Great
Britain: its nature, causes and
problems,**
1980. Report prepared for the
European Centre for Work and
Society, Utrecht.
A recent study for the EOC found
that hourly rates were equal for
full and part time workers in 87%
of establishments.
See A McIntosh, 'Women at
Work: a survey of employers'
Employment Gazette,
November, 1980, p.1142-1149
10
DE,
'Patterns of Pay: Early Results of
the NES',
Employment Gazette,
October, 1980, p.1090
11
S Shimmin et al, op cit, 1981

12
ACAS,
Report No.13,
1978, para 7.12, p.39
13
Commission on Industrial
Relations,
Report no 77,
1973, para 179, p.46
14
S Crine,
The Hidden Army,
Low Pay Unit, 1979
15
C Hakim, op cit, 1980, p.1107
16
DE,
Employment Gazette,
March, 1982, table 5.4 (UK
figures)
17
R Layard et al, op cit, 1978,
p.90
18
National Board of Prices and
Incomes, op cit, 1970
19
C Fudge,
'Night and Day'
Employment Gazette,
October, 1980, p.1121
20
DE,
'Patterns of Pay, op cit, 1980,
p.1090
21
R Layard et al, op cit, 1978.
p.90
22
DHSS, unpublished data on
receipt of FIS amongst families
with both parents in work is
available though not regularly
published. In April 1981 they
represented around 6 per cent
of total FIS awards (figures based
on DHSS six monthly analysis of
a 10 per cent sample of FIS
awards). It is also interesting to
note that in April 1980 75 per
cent of FIS recipients had
earnings above the tax threshold
when benefit was claimed
(Hansard, 9 April, 1981, col.314).
23
House of Commons Hansard,
Written Answers,
9 July 1981, col. 210
24
W W Daniel, op cit, 1981, p.viii.4

103

25
D Smith, op cit, 1981, p.61

26
See for example the discussion
by A Walker,
'The level and distribution of
unemployment', p.7-30, in L
Burghes and R Lister (eds),
**Unemployment: Who Pays the
Price?**
CPAG, 1981

27
In particular W W Daniel, op cit,
1981, and S Moylan and B
Davies, op cit, 1980, p.831

28
S Moylan and B Davies, op cit,
1980, p.832

29
C Smee and J Stern, op cit,
1978, p.14

30
R Layard et al, op cit, 1978

31
DHSS,
Social Security Statistics 1980
HMSO, 1981, Table 46.15

32
D Piachaud,
'Social Security, in N Bosanquet
and P Townsend (eds),
Labour and Equality,
Heinemann, 1980, p.178

33
S Parker,
Older Workers and Retirement,
OPCS Social Survey Division
HMSO, 1980, p.20

34
M Rowland (ed),
**Rights Guide to Non Means
Tested Social Security Benefits,**
4th Edition, CPAG, 1981

35
DHSS,
'More Mothers to Get Maternity
Grant',
Press Release 82/87, 1 April, 1982

36
Quoted in R Elliott et al,
**Women in the Labour Market:
a study of the impact of
legislation and policy towards
women in the UK labour market
during the 1970s,**
paper prepared for the
International Institute of
Management, Berlin, 1981, p.173

37
W W Daniel, op cit, 1980, p.35

38
ibid, p.118

39
SBC, op cit, 1980

40
House of Commons Hansard
998, 2 February 1981, col.

41
DHSS,
**Claimants to Unemployment
Benefit: Summary of Half
Statistics,** May 1980

42
DHSS,
**Which Benefit? Sixty Ways
Get Cash Help,**
FB2/November 1981

43
SBC, op cit, 1980

44
M Fogarty,
**Retirement Age and Retirement
Costs,** PSI, 1980

45
RCDIW,
Report no 8,
HMSO, 1979, para. 14.17,
et seq.

46
A McIntosh, op cit, 1980,

47
R Layard et al, op cit, 1978

48
ibid, p.125

49
Cmnd 8271,
**Improved Protection for the
Occupational Pension Rights
Expectations of Early Leavers**
Report of the Occupational
Pensions Board, HMSO, 19

50
W W Daniel, op cit, 1980,

51
A Gordon and G Williams,
**Attitudes of Fifth and Sixth
Formers to School, Work and
Higher Education,**
University of Lancaster, Report
to the Department of Education
and Science, 1977

52
ibid, p.110

53
Personal communication,

54
Government Statistical Service
**Education Statistics for the
United Kingdom, 1979,**
1982, Table 49, p.56

55
The Community Enterprise Programme provides temporary work for 18-24 year olds (who have been unemployed for six months or more) for a one year period. Though the upper age limit for YOP is now 24 the major focus of the programme is the younger school leaver.

56
Youthaid,
Bulletin,
No. 1, December, 1981

57
This figure is described in the White Paper as approximate. The precise figure will be decided nearer the date in 1983 when the scheme comes into full operation

58
Department of Employment,
A New Training Initiative: A Programme for Action,
HMSO, 1981

59
ibid, and Youthaid
Bulletin,
No.2, February, 1982

60
DE,
Employment Gazette,
HMSO, September, 1980, Table 1 p.1008

61
J Robinson,
'Cervical Cancer: A Feminist Critique',
Times Health Supplement,
no.5, 1981, p.16

62
DHSS, Low Incomes in 1979 (1979 FES data), unpublished mimeo.

63
See for example various editions of the General Household Survey

64
G Brown and T Harris,
Social Origins of Depression: A Study of Psychiatric Disorders in Women,
Tavistock, London, 1978

65
A Marsh, op cit, 1979

66
GMWU, op cit, 1980

67
See for example J Harrington,
Shiftwork and Health, a critical review of the literature,
Health and Safety Executive and HMSO, 1978

68
P J Taylor and S Pocock,
'Mortality of Shift and Day Workers 1956-1968',
British Journal of Industrial Medicine,
29, 1972, p.201-207

69
TGWU,
Stress At Work,
Trade Union Resource and Information Centre, Leeds, 1981

70
F Robertson Elliott,
Occupational Commitments and Paternal Deprivation in Children: Care, Health and Development, 4,
1978, p.305-315

71
Soldiers', Sailors' and Airmen's Families Association,
SSAFA News,
Summer 1980, p.3

72
A Marsh, op cit, 1979

73
S Shimmin et al, op cit, 1981, p.348

74
C Fudge, op cit, 1980

75
For a discussion of research in this field see D Tasto, M Colligan, E Skjei and S Polly, 1978, 'Health Consequences of Shiftwork', US Department of Health, Education and Welfare, Project no URU 4426.

76
ibid

77
C Cooper,
'Coronaries: the risks to the working mother',
Times.
17 December, 1980 and
Trends in Morality 1951-1975 England and Wales,
OPCS Series DHI, No. 3, 1978.

78
National Heart Lung and Blood Institute, Framingham Heart Study, quoted in C Cooper, op cit 1980

79
S Shimmin et al, op cit, 1981
80
A Cragg and T Dawson, op cit, 1981, See also F Field, **Seventy Years On: A New Report on homeworking,** TUC, 1980
81
See for example, the report of the Haringey working party on homeworking and child care, June 1980, and **Health and Safety Executive, FI note, 1980/77,** 'Decision of Court of Summary Jurisdiction for first case under the Health and Safety at Work Act 1974 to involve homeworkers'
82
A Cragg nd T Dawson, op cit, 1981, p.23
83
S Rosenfield, 1980, 'Sex differences in depression: do women always have higher rates?', **Journal of Health and Social Behaviour, 21,** 1980, p.33-42
84
R Cochrane and M Stopes-Roe, 'Women, Marriage, Employment and Mental Health', **British Journal of Psychiatry, 139** p.373-381, 1981
85
L Stolz, 'Effects of Maternal Employment on Children: Evidence from Research', **Child Development, 31,** 1960, p.749-782.
86
R Davie, N Butler and H Goldstein, **From Birth to Seven,** Longman in association with National Children's Bureau, 1972
87
See 'Findings', **New Society,** 23 April 1981, p.44
88
M Rutter, **Maternal Deprivation Reassessed,** Penguin, 1972

89
M McDowall, P Goldblatt and Fox, 'Employment During Pregnancy and Infant Mortality', **Population Trends 26,** 1981, p.12-15
90
Commission of the European Communities, **The Europeans And Their Children,** Brussels, 1979, p.32
91
CPRS, op cit, 1980, para 6.1
92
C Smee and J Stern, op cit, 1
93
See for example L Fagin, **Unemployment and Health in Families,** DHSS, 1981 and J Hartley an Cooper. 'Redundancy: A Psychological Problem?' **Personnel Review** vol 5, no 3, 1976.
94
L Fagin, op cit, 1982, and S 'Social Support as a Moderat Life Stress', **Psychosomatic Medicine,** 1976, 38, p.5
95
In addition to the work of L Fagin, 1980, ibid, research is presently being conducted in the effects of unemploymen women workers, by, for exam C Callender at Cardiff Univer and on the family by, for exa L McKee and C Bell at Aston University.
96
For a summary of the findin and methods of early major studies in this field see P Eisenberg and P Lazarsfield, 'The Psychological Effects of Unemployment', **Psychological Bulletin,** 1938, 35, p.358-90. See also J Stern, **Unemployment and Its Impa Morbidity and Mortality, Ce for Labour Economics Disc Paper no 93,** London School of Economi 1981

97
H Gravelle, G Hutchinson and J Stern,
Mortality and Unemployment: A Cautionary Note',
Centre for Labour Economics Discussion Paper no 95, London School of Economics, 1981
98
A Walker, op cit, 1981
99
G Stokes, unpublished PhD Thesis, Birmingham University, Department of Psychology, 1980
100'
ibid
101
L Fagin, op cit, 1981
102
S Cobb and S Kasl,
The Consequences of Job Loss,
NIOSH Research Report, US Department of Health, Education and Welfare, Publication No. 77-224
103
See for example, L Iverson and H Klausen,
Lukingen af Nordharns-Vaerflet,
Institut for Social Medicin, Kobenhauns Universitet, Publication 13, 1981
104
N Madge,
'Unemployment and its Effects on Children',
Journal of Child Psychology and Psychiatry, forthcoming, 1982
105
L Fagin, op cit, 1981
106
J Douglas,
The Home and the School,
MacGibbon and Kee, 1964
and
J Douglas, J Ross and H Simpson,
All our Future: a longitudinal study of secondary education,
Peter Davies, 1968
107
M Brennan and B Stoten,
'Children, poverty and illness',
New Society,
36, 1976, p.681-2
108
J Carter and P Easton, 1980,
'Separation and other stress in child care,' Lancet, i, p.972-3.

109
There is very little research evidence in this field. Some qualitative material has been collected during a small Manpower Services funded Research Project in Cornwall, Newcastle and SE London (INTO WORK), whilst organisations dealing with young people, such as YMCA and the Samaritans are expressing their concern through annual reports, for example.
110
J Tunnard,
Unemployment — Family Stress and Public Care,
Paper presented to the Consultation on Unemployment and the Family organised by the Family Forum and available from the Family Rights Group.
111
Quoted in the
Daily Telegraph,
18 September 1980

IV. CONCLUSION

1
OPCS, op cit, 1981, p.77
2
A Hunt, op cit, 1968, p.183
3
C Rossiter,
Women, Work and the Family: a report on a survey of 'Townswoman' readers,
Study Commission on the Family, 1980
4
OPCS, op cit, 1980a
5
EOC, op cit, 1980
6
OECD,
The Welfare State in Crisis,
OECD, 1981, p.6